Interdisciplinary Learning Series

Domestic to Interpersonal Violence

An Interdisciplinary Approach

Volume One

Risk Factors, Warning Signs, and Diagnosis

Interdisciplinary Learning Series

STM **Learning,** Inc.

Leading Publisher of Scientific, Technical, and Medical Educational Resources

Saint Louis

www.stmlearning.com

STM *Learning,* Inc.

We've partnered with Copyright Clearance Center for you to conveniently request permissions.

For rights to reproduce content from this title, please visit **www.copyright.com**. Additional requests can be sent directly to **info@copyright.com**.

For more information, please visit **www.stmlearning.com** or email **orders@stmlearning.com**.

About Copyright Clearance Center

Copyright Clearance Center (CCC), the rights licensing expert, is a global rights broker for the world's most sought-after books, journals, blogs, movies, and more. Founded in 1978 as a not-for-profit organization, CCC provides smart solutions that simplify the access and licensing of content that lets businesses and academic institutions quickly get permission to share copyright-protected materials, while compensating publishers and creators for the use of their works. We make copyright work. For more information, visit ***www.copyright.com***

Domestic to Interpersonal Violence

An Interdisciplinary Approach

Volume One

Risk Factors, Warning Signs, and Diagnosis

Interdisciplinary Learning Series

Jaclyn Rodriguez, BSN, BS, RN, SANE-A, SANE-P
CEO
ForMed Insight, LLC
Sexual Assault Nurse Examiner
Endeavor Health and Northwestern Medicine
Libertyville, Illinois

Tamara A. Jackson, MSN, RN, SANE-A, SANE-P
System SANE Program Manager
Emergency Department
Sinai Chicago Health System
Chicago, Illinois

Laura Albee, MD
Emergency Physician
Medical Director for Heidi Wilke SANE/SART Survivor Program
Medical Director for HEAL Omaha, Street Medicine Program
Omaha, Nebraska

STM **Learning,** Inc.

Leading Publisher of Scientific, Technical, and Medical Educational Resources
Saint Louis
www.stmlearning.com

Publishers: Glenn E. Whaley and Marianne V. Whaley
Managing Editor: Samantha Brown
Graphic Design Director: Glenn E. Whaley
Graphic Designer: Connie H. C. Wang
Curriculum Developer: Samantha Brown
Associate Editors: Megan Farmer, Katie Slaten, Miya Russell, Gracie York, Tammy Arnow
Copy Editors: Megan Farmer, Katie Slaten, Miya Russell, Gracie York, Tammy Arnow

Printed in the United States of America.

Publisher:
STM Learning, Inc.
Saint Louis, Missouri 63033
Phone: (314) 434-2424
http://www.stmlearning.com orders@stmlearning.com

Library of Congress Control Number: 2025935132

Print ISBN: 978-1-953119-14-8
eBook ISBN: 978-1-953119-15-5

Contributors

Laura Albee, MD
Emergency Physician
Medical Director for Heidi Wilke SANE/SART Survivor Program
Medical Director for HEAL Omaha, Street Medicine Program
Omaha, Nebraska

Terri Augspurger, MSN, RN, AFN-BC, SANE-A, SANE-P
Forensic Healthcare Program Manager
NMRTC/NH Jacksonville Department of Defense
Clinical Forensic Nurse Examiner
Directorate of Medical Services
Department of Defense
Jacksonville, Florida

Catherine J. Carter-Snell, PhD, RN, SANE-A, DF-AFN
Professor
School of Nursing and Midwifery
Mount Royal University
Calgary, Alberta, Canada

Margit B. Gerardi, PhD, APRN, WHNP, PMHNP-BC
Nurse Practitioner
Mental Health Nurse Practitioner Residency Program Director
Department of Psychiatry
Veterans Administration
Adjunct Assistant Professor
School of Nursing
University of Texas Health Science Center at San Antonio
Recurring Faculty
School of Nursing
Texas Tech University
San Antonio, Texas

Tamara A. Jackson, MSN, RN, SANE-A, SANE-P
System SANE Program Manager
Emergency Department
Sinai Chicago Health System
Chicago, Illinois

Kate Lawler, MPH
System Vice President of Community Impact and Engagement
Endeavor Health
Chicago, Illinois

Catherine Mortiere, PhD
Licensed Psychologist
Department of Psychology
Kirby Forensic Psychiatric Center
Clinical Instructor
Department of Psychiatry
New York University School of Medicine
New York, New York

Tracie L. Nicolai, PhD, EdD
Nationally Certified School Psychologist

Michelle Ortiz, MSN, RN, AFN-BC, SANE-A, IPVNE, SAMFE
Forensic Healthcare Coordinator
Naval Medical Center
Defense Health Agency
Department of Defense
Portsmouth, Virginia

Jaclyn Rodriguez, BSN, BS, RN, SANE-A, SANE-P
CEO
ForMed Insight, LLC
Sexual Assault Nurse Examiner
Endeavor Health and Northwestern Medicine
Libertyville, Illinois

Tracy G. Senterfitt, MSN, APRN, PMHNP-BC
Psychiatric Mental Health Nurse Practitioner
Department of Psychiatry
Veterans Healthcare System
San Antonio, Texas

Amy Taylor Signore, DNP, MSN, BS, RN, SANE-A, SANE-P
Sexual Assault Nurse Examiner Team Lead
Emergency Department
Sexual Assault Nurse Examiner Department
Hospital Sisters Health System St. Elizabeth's Hospital
Adjunct Professor
Nursing Education Department
Southwestern Illinois College
Belleville, Illinois

Richard Sochor

Jen Tran, MSN, RN, SANE-A
Forensic Nurse Examiner
Methodist Health System
Omaha, Nebraska

Olivia Yeargain, MPH, MSN, APRN, PMHNP-BC
Psychiatric Mental Health Nurse Practitioner
Department of Psychiatry
Veterans Administration
San Antonio, Texas

Amy Zabel, BSN, RN, SANE-A, RNC-MNN, IPVNE, LCDR, ANC
Forensic Nurse Examiner Instructor
United States Nurse Corps
United States Navy
San Antonio, Texas

Our Mission

To become the world leader in publishing and information services on child abuse, maltreatment, diseases, and domestic violence. We seek to heighten awareness of these issues and provide relevant information to professionals and consumers.

Foreword

What is it that survivors of domestic violence need from us to support them in escaping an abusive situation? Access to safety. Access to knowledge. Access to resources. By emphasizing the need for access to safety, knowledge, and resources, we highlight the critical gaps that many survivors face. It is crucial that each of us recognizes that the barriers to achieving safety and self-sufficiency can stem from both individual people choosing to cause harm and systemic barriers facing communities. Advocating for supportive networks and ensuring that resources are available and accessible can and will make a significant difference in the lives of those affected. We are stronger together as we work towards closing these gaps and creating a more supportive community for survivors and their children.

It is crucial to recognize that those who cause harm are often strategic in their actions, deliberately isolating their partners to maintain control. They often manipulate information and restrict access to resources, effectively cutting off any avenues for support. This calculated approach not only creates immediate barriers but also impacts a survivor's ability to build, or rebuild, a safe future. Understanding these dynamics is essential for communities and support networks. By raising awareness about the tactics of manipulation and coercive control, we can better equip ourselves to recognize the signs of abuse and offer meaningful support. Empowering survivors means not only providing resources but also fostering environments where they feel safe to seek help without fear of retribution. It is vital to challenge these harmful behaviors and create spaces that promote healing, safety, and empowerment.

Regardless of the unique obstacles each survivor faces, it is essential that our support systems are constructed to provide survivors flexibility by breaking down the barriers and red tape that survivors often have break through, whether that is through court to access to legal protections, through Child Protective Services, or even finding affordable housing. It is critical that each of us, no matter our role, are prepared to tailor our own responses to a survivor's individual needs. Communities should not only offer resources but listen to survivors' experiences and validate their journeys. By embracing the diversity of each story, we can create a more inclusive approach that can allow survivors to feel empowered to assess their options and make informed decisions about what is best for themselves and their children. Our collective goal should be to foster collaborative environments that intentionally dismantle systemic oppression like racism and homophobia, where survivors feel understood and supported, allowing them to envision and pursue a future free from abuse; a future where they can thrive and where their children can thrive. Every effort we make to celebrate and accommodate these differences strengthens our collective ability to support those in need of our help. Together, we must work to pave those pathways to safety and healing.

Sarah Conlon (she/her/hers)
Interim President/CEO
Illinois Coalition Against Domestic Violence

FOREWORD

Preface

This workbook has been crafted for a diverse audience including new and experienced sexual assault nurse examiners (SANEs), sexual assault forensic examiners (SAFEs), first responders including emergency medical service and law enforcement, nurse practitioners, physician assistants, medical residents, physicians, nursing students, advocates, and attorneys. In this 3-volume workbook we strive to increase your knowledge base regarding interpersonal violence and provide a framework for you to guide people who are experiencing a violent or controlling relationship.

Terminology has evolved over the years from domestic violence (DV) to intimate partner violence (IPV) to interpersonal violence and relationship violence. For this text, we primarily use the term "interpersonal violence" to incorporate all types of relationship violence. You may notice quotes and historical references throughout the text which use the older terminology.

The primary objective of this resource is to establish a standardized language ensuring uniformity and coherence in program development across various agencies. By providing a common framework, this resource aims to enhance communication, foster collaboration, and ultimately improve the quality of care and support for survivors of interpersonal violence.

We recognize that interpersonal violence can occur in all types of relationships including heterosexual, homosexual, parent-child, and teen dating through advanced age. We have specific chapters to address LGBTQIA+ concerns and military circumstances. We understand that interpersonal violence can be perpetrated by women as well as men. To keep the writing concise, we do not always differentiate between same-sex or heterosexual relationships, but we remember that the concepts presented in this text can apply to all relationships.

Volume 1 focuses on how to recognize and understand interpersonal violence. We provide an overview of the issue as well as historical perspectives on how society evolved to our current situations regarding interpersonal violence. Types of abuse included in this text include physical, sexual, and emotional/psychological which includes stalking. We expand on these types of abuse as well as risk factors for relationships that involve interpersonal violence.

The chapter addressing LGBTQIA+ issues offers an extensive list of definitions to be aware of when working with this community. There are special considerations when interpersonal violence occurs in a military setting. In the health care setting hospitals and clinics are in a unique position to recognize and offer intervention for people experiencing interpersonal violence. This requires a multidisciplinary team who are educated to provide trauma-informed care. We attempt to provide a framework to help you build and improve these systems within health care settings. Interpersonal violence can lead to long-lasting emotional and physical repercussions for survivors and their families. We also address the far-reaching impacts which include economic and societal costs.

Thank you for investing in Volume 1. We hope that you are able to apply this information in your professional practice. In Volume 2, we take an in-depth look at the physical and psychological impacts of interpersonal violence on survivors. Volume 3 tackles opportunities for treatment, prevention, and legal intervention. We hope that this workbook series helps you expand your understanding of interpersonal violence and provides opportunities for you to offer meaningful support and hope to survivors.

Laura Albee, MD
Emergency Physician
Medical Director for Heidi Wilke SANE/SART Survivor Program
Medical Director for HEAL Omaha, Street Medicine Program
Omaha, Nebraska

Reviews

Providing trauma-informed, evidence-based care to domestic violence survivors involves considering many perspectives from different disciplines and integrating them all into a thorough assessment. Domestic to Interpersonal Violence *lays the groundwork for understanding the many facets that are included in building a robust domestic violence assessment practice for clinicians. The comprehensive nature of the text, going all the way into a historical perspective and societal perceptions of domestic violence, shows the amount of care that was taken to ensure a well-rounded approach regarding the nuances and complexities of assessing survivors of domestic violence. Practitioners with all levels of experience will benefit greatly from this workbook!*

Brenda Ireland, BSN, RN, SANE-A, SANE-P
She/Her/Hers
SANE Coordinator
Pediatric Quality Coordinator
Emergency Department RN
OSF Saint Joseph Medical Center
Bloomington, IL

This is a valuable text for anyone who provides care to domestic violence survivors. It covers all aspects of not only care for the victim but also insight into legal matters and how to assure that evidence is not lost or compromised. It provides background into the social and economic aspects of domestic violence and information on how to help survivors navigate these difficult situations. The text highlights best practices and provides practical advice for setting up these practices in the everyday health care setting.

Anke Horacek, MD
Emergency Medicine Physician
Omaha, Nebraska

Domestic to Interpersonal Violence *examines the course of how a domestic relationship becomes intimate partner violence over the lifespan of the victims and the potential impact it can have along the way. From pregnancy to fatality, domestic violence can impact women and the children who witness or experience domestic violence in the home by child maltreatment and intergenerational transmission of violence. The impact to the victims can include contracting sexually transmitted infections (STIs), sexual assault, suicide, substance abuse, and other mental health deterioration such as post-traumatic stress disorder (PTSD), depression, and eating disorders. In the extreme forms, it leads to strangulation, head injuries, and eventually death. This volume highlights these dangers along with risk factors to intimate partner violence and barriers the victims face. Each chapter gives ways to intervene in hopes of changing the course of outcome for the women, children, and men living in their world of chaos and fear.*

Tracie L. Nicolai, PhD, EdD
Nationally Certified School Psychologist

Domestic to Interpersonal Violence *is an essential resource that offers a comprehensive exploration of domestic violence, its historical roots, and its complex impact on individuals and society. Through well-researched chapters, the text provides critical insights into the evolution of societal attitudes, the intersection of domestic violence with public health, and the importance of intervention strategies. The book's interdisciplinary approach ensures that readers—from health care providers to policymakers—gain a nuanced understanding of both survivors and perpetrators. By emphasizing evidence-based assessment and intervention techniques, this text is an invaluable tool for those dedicated to addressing and preventing domestic violence in all its forms.*

Paul Thomas Clements, PhD, RN, AFN-C
Board Certified Advanced Practice Forensic Nurse
Clinical Professor
Texas A&M University Center for Excellence in Forensic Nursing

Contents in Brief

Contents in Detail

Domestic to Interpersonal Violence

An Interdisciplinary Approach

Volume One

Risk Factors, Warning Signs, and Diagnosis

Interdisciplinary Learning Series

STM **Learning,** Inc.

Leading Publisher of Scientific, Technical, and Medical Educational Resources

Saint Louis

www.stmlearning.com

Section I

Risk Factors, Warning Signs, and Diagnosis

Chapter 1

Interpersonal Violence: *An Overview of the Problem*

Catherine J. Carter-Snell, PhD, RN, SANE-A, DF-AFN

Objectives

After reviewing this chapter, the reader will be able to:

1. *Describe interpersonal violence terms, types, and the scope.*
2. *Discuss the adverse effects (physical and psychological) for those experiencing interpersonal violence, including possible signs.*
3. *Describe risk and protective factors for interpersonal violence, using a social-ecological model.*
4. *Explore common models used to explain abusive behaviors associated with interpersonal violence, including Johnson's typology, the cycle of violence, and the power and control wheel.*
5. *Describe basic prevention and intervention concepts, including principles of trauma-informed care.*

Introduction

Violence of any form—emotional, psychological, physical, or sexual—is never justified. When it is committed by someone known to the individual, it adds a layer of betrayal and distrust. The psychological and physical harm caused by the abuse can have long-term effects. The focus of this series is to provide an in-depth understanding of abuse that occurs in the context of a current or previous relationship. This includes an understanding of the risk factors for violence, either as a victim/survivor or someone with abusive behavior, models that help explain the violence, and the adverse effects of violence on peoples' lives.

Terminology

There are many terms used when discussing abuse in a relationship, past or present. The term ***domestic violence*** is common but does not resonate with some who are not cohabiting or dating, or who are experiencing violence from previous partners. Youth in violent dating relationships also do not see themselves included in the term. Throughout this book, the term ***interpersonal violence*** will be used. This is because not all relationships are seen as intimate or between partners. In addition, it may be interpreted that the abuse is of an intimate or sexual nature, but other forms of abuse may still occur (eg, emotional or psychological). As a result, the terms ***intimate partner violence*** (IPV) and ***relationship violence*** may also be encountered in the literature. There are many forms of interpersonal violence, which may include child abuse, bullying, relationship abuse, and elder abuse.

The terms used for the types of interpersonal violence also vary. Common categories include physical violence, sexual violence, stalking, and psychological aggression.[1] Other terms may also be encountered such as financial abuse, spiritual abuse, reproductive coercion, coercive control, and technology-facilitated violence or cyber-violence.[2] Furthermore, legal terms may impact understanding of factors such as sexual violence. In Canada, any contact of a sexual nature without consent is sexual assault and may include coercion, withholding of contraception, or being forced to watch pornography.[3] In the United States, the term "rape" is used but typically is seen as referring to vaginal/penile penetration and in some cases does not include objects other than the penis, or does not include men.[4] The statutes are described as differing in each state, and some have either expanded their definition of "rape" or added "sexual assault" legislation. An understanding of the elements included in legislation, definitions, acts included, source of data, as well as the context of questions used, is important when comparing regional, national, or even international data.

Reporting of interpersonal violence is another issue. This varies across countries and even between states or provinces and depends on circumstances such as immediate threat to life for the patient or others and the presence of children witnessing the violence. Factors such as physical or psychological injury and harm, and severe forms of physical violence such as strangulation, will affect the level of charges brought by police in almost all jurisdictions.

There is often discomfort as to how to refer to the person being abused and the person abusing. Social workers typically use the term "survivor," however nurses will typically use the term "patient," as they are seeing them during physical treatment before the person moves into a survivor phase. Many clients do not like to be defined by their trauma, but avoiding the term "victim" to some feels like others are minimizing the trauma. For this chapter, the term "victim" will sometimes be used for ease of explanation. It is preferred that care professionals call them a "client" or "patient" in most communication if providing health care, especially if care professionals go to court as expert witnesses—referring to them as a victim or survivor may suggest bias to medical findings. As for the person perpetrating the abuse, the preference is to avoid calling them an "abuser" and instead, refer to the behavior (eg, the person abusing, or the person with abusive behavior).

Impact of Interpersonal Violence

Scope of the Problem

The variety of terms make comparisons of data difficult between countries, as does the source of the data, such as police-reported and population-level survey data. Despite these data challenges, it is clear that the scope of interpersonal violence is significant. A global population-level study of 161 countries found that almost 1/3 of women worldwide have been physically or sexually abused by a current or former intimate partner.[5] Youth data are also important to include, as interpersonal violence can begin at an early age, around when dating begins.[6] The age group at highest risk for IPV is between 22 and 44 years, but approximately 25% of women and 18% of men under 18 years have experienced physical or sexual violence or stalking by an intimate partner.[5,7] Youth who identify as a sexual or cultural minority are at higher risk than others.[7-9] Physical abuse was experienced by 23% of women, compared to 17% of men, psychological abuse by 43% of women versus 35% of men, and sexual abuse much more by women, 12% versus 2%. National American survey data indicate that 1 in 4 women and 1 in 10 men experience IPV, including physical or sexual forms of abuse.[10]

Adverse Effects

The consequences of interpersonal violence are significant and potentially long-lasting, as well as cumulative and intergenerational. When the stress response system in the brain is severely or repetitively activated, the resulting changes in the brain contribute to the development of post-traumatic stress disorder (PTSD).[11] More severe or repetitive experiences with IPV have been linked to the severity of PTSD, depression, and chronic pain.[12] Women with past experiences of IPV have been recognized as at high risk for PTSD, depression, and anxiety.[13] While women's PTSD and physical health symptoms were described as often more severe and long-lasting than men's, national data showed that male victims of IPV experienced worse overall mental health outcomes.[14] Other consequences include substance abuse, decreases in academic achievement or job performance, and suicidal ideation.[15,16] The experience of IPV can also affect future relationships and attachments.[17,18] In addition to PTSD, stress can alter the formation of memories, the ability to put remaining memories into order, and may even affect the ability to speak while stressed,[19] all of which impact others' belief of the experience(s) and victims' likelihood of reporting. The partner experiencing abuse typically becomes reliant on their partner due to the partner's use of progressive attacks on their self-esteem, increasing isolation, and creation of fear. The result may be "harmed identity," in which the victim blames themselves, tries to manage their own behavior to reduce outbursts, and gradually develops feelings of disempowerment and entrapment.[20] There are also risks to leaving the relationship in some cases, and abused individuals may refuse to leave or to press charges and are likely to return to the abusive relationship many times before they are able to break free.[21] Behaviors such as avoidance, harmed identity, shame and self-blame, memory gaps, and mental health disorders or substance abuse affect the believability of the victim and likelihood of prosecution.

Physical injury can be a consequence of interpersonal violence. Traumatic brain injury has been found in 19% to 100% of victims experiencing IPV.[22] Victims may also experience injuries from blunt or penetrating mechanisms, being shaken, or from self-harm.[23] Injury patterns suggesting interpersonal violence are somewhat difficult to determine, due to a variety of factors including variability in terminology used, examiner skill and technique, as well as skin color.[24-26] Some patterns of injury have emerged regardless of these challenges. Data indicate that the violence experienced by women more often includes severe forms of violence, including attempted strangulations, assaults with a weapon or sustaining severe physical or psychological harm, forced sex, threats of harm to a pet, and death.[2,27] If the violence occurs during pregnancy, it is associated with greater risks of small birthweight babies, delayed perinatal care, more perinatal complications including death, and poorer health for both mother and child.[28]

There is substantial evidence to link the psychological consequences of violence to chronic and long-term physical health issues. A systematic review of research conducted on the Nurses' Health Study II identified that trauma at any stage of life, such as interpersonal violence, negatively impacted physical health, especially if PTSD symptoms were present.[29] Women experiencing sexual violence with penetration and those being stalked by men had the most health conditions in a regression analysis of the American National Relationship Violence and Sexual Violence Survey.[10,30] A dose-dependent relationship was noted, meaning that as the number and types of IPV increased, the prevalence of adverse health conditions increased.[30]

Witnessing IPV as a child is considered one of the Adverse Childhood Experiences (ACEs).[31] ACEs are closely linked to many diseases and risks of other forms of abuse, particularly if appropriate support systems are not available. Witnessing IPV as a child has also been found to be a stronger contributor to adult PTSD, even more than abuse experiences as an adult or adolescent.[32]

Risks for Interpersonal Violence

The social-ecological model,[33] which was originally developed as the ecological model for the World Health Organization by Dahl and Krug, is a useful guide to discussions of risks and subsequent prevention or intervention planning. The model has also been adopted by the Centers for Disease Control and Prevention and applied to interpersonal violence (**Figure 1-1**). The model shows the interconnectedness between different levels of risks, with implications for different levels of prevention.

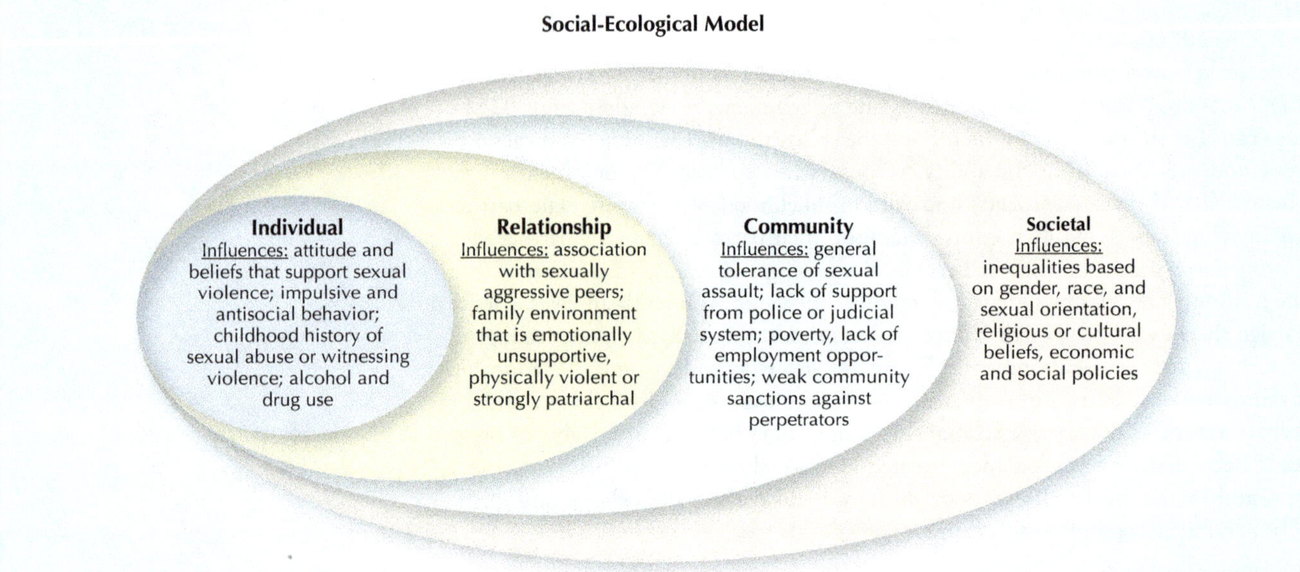

Figure 1-1

Figure 1-1. *Social-Ecological Model. (public domain: CDC http://www.cdc.gov/violenceprevention/pdf/SVPrevention-a.pdf)*

Many factors can influence risks for interpersonal violence. Younger women, as well as sexual and ethnic minorities, are high-risk as they are considered to have less power and are more marginalized. Other individual risk factors include lower levels of education and income, which are interrelated,[34] as well as substance abuse.[35] Pregnancy may also be a risk, with 1/4 of pregnant women worldwide having experienced IPV.[36] It is not clear whether the higher prevalence is due to abuse commencing during pregnancy, increasing, or whether women decide to disclose at this time. The nature of the pregnancy may also be a factor, especially if it is unplanned or unwanted in the relationship.[34] Members of the LGBTQIA+ community are at particularly high risk of IPV as well as other forms of victimization.[2,37] A national American study identified that almost 1/2 of transgender adults had experienced IPV, especially trans men who were low-income with limited education, and who engaged in sex work or substance abuse.[38] These individual risk factors, including intersectionality, help to understand risks for interpersonal violence and targeting strategies for prevention or intervention efforts.

Men report experiencing IPV at almost the same rates as women, although almost 80% of those reporting IPV to police identify as female.[39] Men's risks for experiencing relationship violence are poorly understood, but some patterns are emerging. Men may experience severe physical abuse but are much less likely to report to police.[40] Some of this is due to fear of disbelief—some men who have tried to report have had police arrest them rather than their female partner.[38] They also report experiencing many barriers to help-seeking,[40,41] including unemployment, living with young children, society not seeing resources as relevant to men, and lack of male shelters. Men are also more likely to both experience abuse and to perpetrate abuse,[42] especially if they have experienced adverse socialization and sexual abuse in childhood. This overlap makes it difficult for them to seek services when some specify men cannot participate if they have ever perpetrated abusive behavior.

Family and peers can also impact risk. In addition to witnessing IPV, ACEs can also include experiencing child maltreatment (physical, sexual, emotional or neglect), having a family member with mental health or substance abuse problems, having someone in the family die by suicide, parental separation, or having someone in the household who is in jail or prison.[43] Children exposed to IPV were more likely to believe that violence in intimate relationships is acceptable, which raises risks for future dating violence.[44] The elderly also experience interpersonal violence, but it is poorly understood in this age group. Abuse in care homes typically must be reported but the majority of elderly remain in their homes, therefore most violence occurs in private. The person with abusive behaviors is often a partner who has been abusive throughout the couple's lifespan.[45] Having experienced prior IPV, either as an ACE or in one's own relationship, is a risk factor for future IPV, especially if the survivor has not received sufficient support after the experience. The nature of the couple's living situation may also make a difference. Cohabiting couples are more at risk than married couples. Income disparity within the relationship may also be an issue, if the husband earns less[46] or if the lower earner or partner did not have equal input about the income use.[47]

Community risk factors include living in a high-crime or high-density neighborhood, one with high levels of unemployment, or which has few connections or supports for each other. Those living in rural areas experience high rates of IPV and revictimization as well, while having less access to resources to assist them.[48,49] The increased risks relate to isolation and thus reduced detection, limited access to technology, limited access to vehicles to leave the area, and risks of disclosure in small communities who are often interconnected. A similar increased risk was found during the COVID-19 pandemic, with stay-at-home orders increasing isolation and stress.[50] Rates of IPV rose, as did the severity of consequences. Young adults not cohabiting also experienced increased relationship stress during the pandemic, including increased coercion to go outside the home[48] and greater conflicts.[51] Stay-at-home orders reduced access to health and counseling services while increasing stressors in the home and further isolating victims.[52] Once restrictions were lifted, rates of violence resumed or exceeded pre-pandemic levels, while the severity, lethality, or complexity of needs increased substantially.

Key Models Related to Interpersonal Violence

It is important to note that relationships characterized by abusive behavior do not start out that way. The abuse typically begins gradually, often as criticisms, insults, or "put-downs." These forms of emotional abuse erode the recipient's self-esteem. The person the abuse is aimed at may even believe they are at fault and begin managing their behavior to avoid abuse.[53] The partner with abusive behavior may make efforts to isolate and control the other person, such as limiting contact with friends or family. Abuse typically escalates from emotional or psychological to threats and physical abuse (eg, hitting, slapping, biting, or kicking). Unwanted sexual contact or violence is considered a significant escalation and a risk for homicide.[54] The existence of a previously loving or enjoyable relationship, riddled with what some refer to as "love bombs," complicates the survivor's willingness to recognize it as abusive and their willingness to leave as they may believe that the relationship will return to that stage.

Typology of Abusive Behavior

A typology of IPV has been developed by Johnson[55] in which 4 types of abusive behavior are described (**Table 1-1**). The use of power and control is seen in the category called ***coercive control*** (formerly called ***intimate terrorism)***. This is the type of abuse most likely to result in severe injury or death, particularly when women are abused.[56,57] It is suggested that these types of abuse may occur on a continuum, with coercive control being the most extreme, and that it, as well as mutual control, result in the most forms of violence and serious injury.[58,59] The relative frequency of these types varies—in the original studies of adults it was not common to see mutual control, but a study of university-aged relationships identified coercive control equally in men and women.[60] Although there are other typologies, Johnson's typology has been studied in numerous populations and has been found to be empirically supported.[61,62]

Table 1-1. Johnson's Typology[55]

Typology	Characteristics
Situational Violence	Anger or outbursts are related to a **situation** (eg, job loss, financial insecurity, health problems) rather than use of power, control, or coercion. May be male or female abuser.
Coercive Control	Partner uses **power, control, or coercion over** another. More often male abusers against females, but females may also use.
Mutual Violent Control	Both partners use **power, control, or coercion** against each other. May be male or female.
Violent Resistance	The person being abused **retaliates or resists** the abuser's control tactics. These are more often women resisting.

Although it is more common to see male-to-female abuse among those reporting interpersonal violence, both may have abusive behavior. The strongest predictor of abusive behavior is a history of prior abuse.[62] Other risks found in the systematic review included childhood victimization, substance use, abusing one's own children, traditional gender roles, mental health disorders, stress, narcissism, depression or PTSD, anxiety and other mental health problems, as well as external locus of control.

Theories of Violent Behavior

There are 2 predominant models of interpersonal violence, the Cycle of Violence and the Power and Control Wheel (**Figure 1-2**). Walker[64] describes a cycle in which tension builds, the abusive behavior occurs, and then is followed by acts of contrition. This is a repetitive cycle and likely to recur. The most successful time to intervene (and the most likely time for them to seek help) is between the explosion and the honeymoon phase. Once the honeymoon phase resumes, the victim sometimes has hope that the relationship will revert to their original relationship—recall that it typically does not start out as overtly abusive.

The Power and Control Wheel (**Figure 1-2**), or Duluth model, was developed to promote understanding of the tactics used in abuse throughout the cycle. This has been used to develop coordinated community interventions for abusers.[65] While the effectiveness of the model for interventions has been criticized,[66] the wheel itself helps to increase understanding of the variety of tactics used to gain power and control that result in physical, emotional, or sexual abuse. While these tactics may be used outside an abusive relationship out of anger or frustration, in an abusive relationship, there is a history, and the recipient of the abuse will hesitate to respond or choose their actions carefully, knowing abuse may result. These tactics are consistent with the coercive control type of abusive behavior or the mutual violent control models of abuse, which are both characterized by use of power and control over another.

Prevention and Intervention

Those experiencing interpersonal violence do not always seek help and some may avoid certain types of help. They may come for treatment, but often it is not obvious that the injuries are related to abuse. They may present with frequent sexually transmitted infections or urinary tract infections, abdominal pain with no known cause, or substance abuse issues. It is common for them to avoid seeking legal services or police, but they often interact with health care and other formal and informal networks.[67] Their help-seeking varies for many reasons including severity of the violence, ethnicity, and prior experiences with seeking help. For these reasons, it is important

Power and Control Wheel

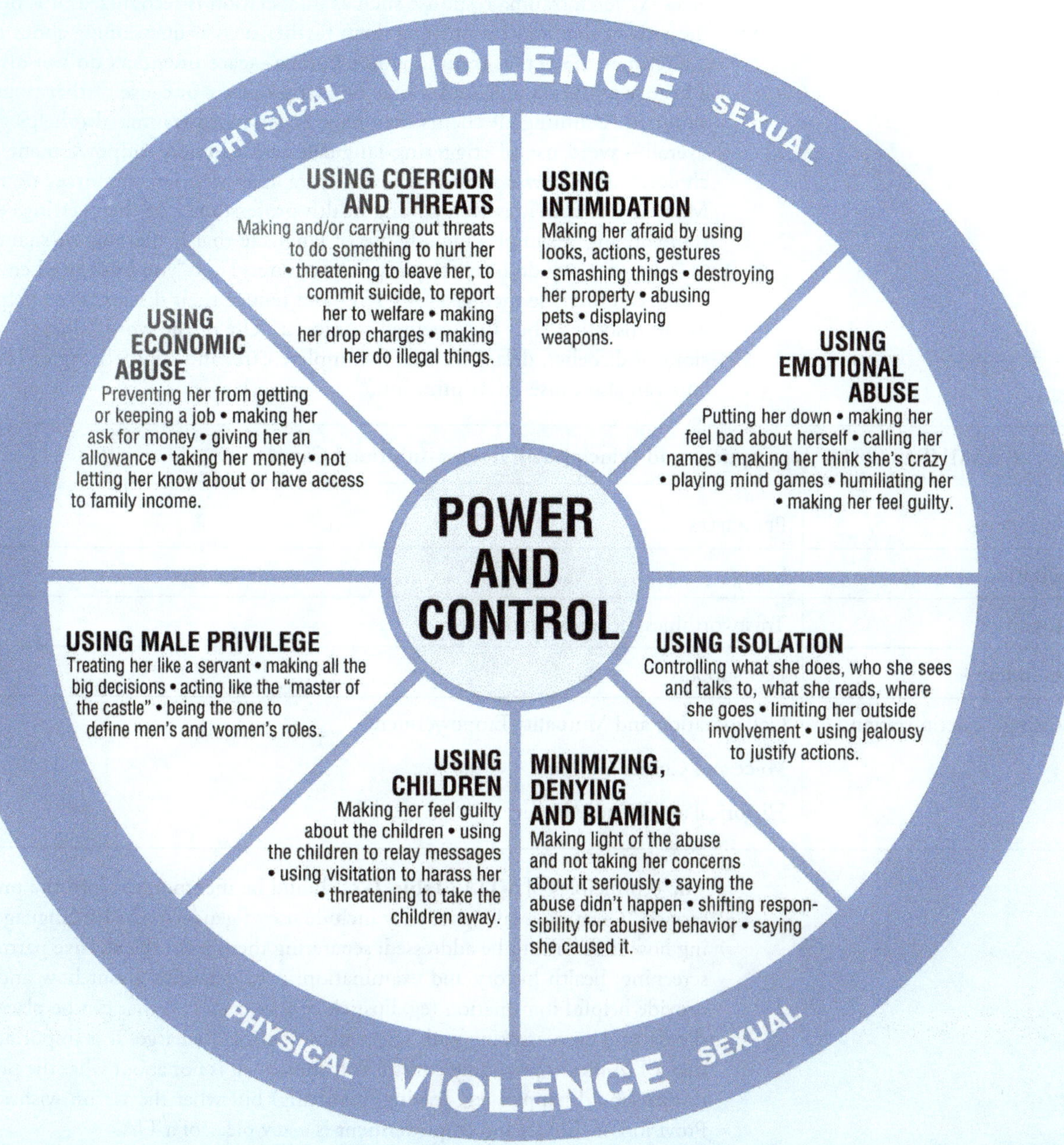

Figure 1-2

Figure 1-2. *Power and Control Wheel. Source: Domestic Violence Intervention Programs (2024) https://www.theduluthmodel.org/wheels/*

for health professionals to screen for interpersonal violence in multiple health care settings. Health care professionals taking steps to help their patient must do so with a trauma-informed approach (TIA) and considering the patient's readiness to change.

Trauma-Informed Approach

The focus of TIA is empowering the individual and restoring control and choice. The discussion of TIA is aided by the use of the key assumptions which include the 4 R's (**Table 1-2**).[68] This chapter, and the entire series, is helpful with the first R: *realization.* Having all providers and administration realize the extent and impact of interpersonal violence and other traumas on health and behavior, as well as the importance of providing sufficient resources and interventions, is essential. *Recognition* of trauma responses, such as dissociation, tonic immobility, and memory and speech issues during provision of services is essential. The *response* is important to prevent further trauma and reduce the person's stress during provision of services. When a trauma response such as dissociation is recognized, it is best to stop the activity that may be stressing them further such as questioning about the abuse. Sometimes the actual trauma is not known—care providers do not always have a history of the trauma, and it may be inappropriate or cause further trauma to ask about it. Assuming all clients may have experienced trauma also helps guide care overall—avoid use of triggering language and promote empowerment of victim choice.[69] ***Revictimization*** can occur from inappropriate resources or responses. Many of the activities seen among health professionals or their settings can be retraumatizing. Examples include use of language that is blaming or shaming, such as "what did you do to make your partner angry?" or "you both need counseling." These can increase their risk of PTSD and reduce their disclosure or help-seeking, as can disbelief: "but they seemed so nice…" Use of the word "alleged" or expressions of disbelief, delays in care, incomplete care, and stigmatizing or labeling clients can also cause revictimization.[70]

Table 1-2. SAMHSA's (2014) Assumptions and Principles of Trauma-Informed Care[68]

Assumptions	Principles
Realization	Safety
Recognition	Trustworthiness & transparency
Responding	Peer support
Resisting Revictimization	Collaboration and Mutuality Empowerment Voice and Choice Cultural Historical and Gender Issues

The 6 principles of a TIA (**Table 1-2**) should be incorporated into the provision of services. Creating a safe space may include use of gender-inclusive language and asking how they wish to be addressed; separating them from the abusive partner for the screening; health history and examination; considerations about how and when to provide helpful information (eg, lipstick containers, cards that can be placed in their shoes); and even assisting with safety planning for discharge. It is important to note that a TIA means providing control and choice—it is not about what the professional thinks should happen (eg, leaving, reporting) but what the victim wishes to occur. Provision of choices and empowerment is a key piece of a TIA.

Screening and Risk Assessment

Screening may be as simple as adding a question to all intakes about whether abuse impacts their life and if so, if they feel safe.[71] Alternatively, it may involve the use of validated screening tools such as the commonly used HITS,[72] which assesses the frequency of being hurt, insulted, threatened, or being screamed at. There are numerous other tools and methods for screening for interpersonal violence. A systematic review of the effectiveness of screening was conducted which indicated sufficient evidence to support screening all women of childbearing age using the more common tools.[73] Effective screening in this group was found to decrease further violence, abuse, and the associated physical and mental consequences. Universal screening has been found to be more effective than selective screening.[70] Some screening tools are available for these populations,[74,75] but more testing and effectiveness studies are needed with larger sample sizes.

Once screening has occurred, if the person affirms violence is an issue, then other tools are typically used to determine the level of risk or need for intervention. The Danger Assessment[54] (**Table 1-3**) is one of the more frequently used tools for intervention. The severity or frequency of each of these factors provides a score to determine risk for lethality. These factors have been incorporated into police risk assessment tools when they respond to calls at a residence. This tool was developed primarily for women experiencing abuse, and its predictive validity for men is not yet established.

Table 1-3. Campbell's Danger Assessment Indicators of Potential Lethality[54]

Factor	Description
Nature of Violence	— Increasing severity or frequency of physical violence — Sexual activity without client's consent
Weapon	— Partner owns a gun — Partner has used a weapon against them or threatened to use it
Lethal Behaviors	— Threats to kill client — Attempts to choke/strangle or cut off breathing — Threatens to harm children
Partner's Behavior	— Use of illegal drugs — Alcoholic or problem drinker — History of prior abusive behavior — Attempts to control client's daily activities — Violently and constantly jealous — Physical abuse of client while pregnant — Threatens to commit suicide
Client's Situation	— Client has left cohabitation within last year — Has a child that is not partner's — Client believes partner is capable of killing them — Client has threatened or tried to commit suicide

There are numerous barriers which result in selective screening.[76,77] Some include limited training, lack of time or management support, inconsistent screening due to stereotypical assumptions about who is likely to have been abused, discomfort asking "personal" questions, or not knowing what to do if the client gives an affirmative response to being abused. Repeated studies of abused women indicate the majority wish they had been asked by professionals, as they see a difference in answering a health professional versus volunteering the information. They may deny the abuse initially, but it may result in reflection and later disclosure. The method of screening is also important. Screening tools that are self-completed by the patient yield greater rates of disclosure than clinician-administered tools.[78] Privacy for these questions is vital. One must also consider the context of the situation, such as, does the history of events match the injuries, are there frequent admissions or visits for health care, is the partner hovering and answering questions on behalf of the client, is there potential fear in responses? Creating space alone with the client is important to explore these suspicions. It is important that care professionals do not push but provide an opening for the client to disclose if they desire.

Effectiveness of Interventions

The complexity of risk factors for interpersonal violence highlights the need for multifaceted prevention and interventional strategies. Evidence for effective interventions is quite limited at present, as studies are quite heterogenous across populations, risk factors, and approaches. A systematic review of family-focused interventions in North America for parental interpersonal violence found a lack of effectiveness, wide variation in approaches, and bias.[79] The variations in approaches, differences in complexity, populations, and even definitions of abuse and perpetrator types may impact the ability to detect effectiveness. For instance, if results of interventions to manage coercive control and situational violence behaviors are pooled, the magnitude of effectiveness may be limited (eg, anger management is not typically effective with coercive control behaviors). Single versus multiple interventions may also influence effectiveness and not reflect the complexity of abuse. The social-ecological model of prevention supports use of multiple interventions in multiple settings.[80] It is also important to improve understanding of the implications of gender on help-seeking and the effectiveness of interventions. There is limited evidence for effectiveness of interventions to prevent abusive behavior or further victimization in men compared to women, and even less in which the types of abusive behaviors are stratified. For instance, a small qualitative study of university-aged male victims of IPV revealed that they were less able to recognize abusive behaviors as IPV or seek help, and did not find existing services to be adequate.[41]

Prevention

The social-ecological model (**Figure 1-1**) previously used to understand risks can also be used to understand and plan prevention strategies. Prevention and early intervention with children exposed to interpersonal violence is a key measure. In addition to gender issues, factors such as income level, pregnancy, and age can also influence the strategies and effectiveness of results.[81] Effectiveness of interpersonal violence interventions in pregnant women were found to be most effective when all levels of the social-ecological model were integrated and varied based on the combination of risk factors.[82] A systematic review of children exposed to interpersonal violence identified emotional intelligence as a positive individual factor, and family level modifiers included positive parenting and family social support, which reduced the negative impacts.[83]

Case Studies

Case Study 1-1

Bradley began dating Madison during their first year of college. Initially, they spent a lot of time together and appeared happy in the relationship. As the school term progressed and academic pressures increased, Bradley wanted to spend more time on his own to catch up with assignments. Madison began to get angry as her assignments piled up. Madison began yelling at Bradley, throwing things at him, and insulting him. She demanded he spend all his spare time with her rather than his friends. His friends began avoiding them because of all the drama. They suggested he just quit making her mad. Bradley suggested that they break up, but Madison threatened to commit suicide if he left her. Eventually, Bradley became more and more withdrawn, and his grades began to drop. He started drinking to cope with his stress. He did poorly on his finals and decided to leave university and return to his hometown. Fortunately, a friend of Bradley's was able to encourage him to seek university counseling services. He had been reluctant to go as he thought the services were only for women and was ashamed to be seen going into the center. He still struggled post-counseling but remained in university.

Discussion

Madison may be displaying the "situational violence" form of abusive behavior. The relationship was relatively smooth until the pressures of reduced income and increased school pressures mounted. This type of abusive behavior may respond well to economic supports, as well as communications and anger management strategies. It could be argued that her threats of suicide are a form of coercive control as is the isolation, so further exploration is warranted.

Bradley was experiencing adverse mental health effects from the abuse and limited informal support; negative informal supports are associated with increased risks of PTSD. This is also demonstrative of societal or community attitudes about interpersonal violence that assume the man is at fault for upsetting the woman. His grades and alcohol abuse may have been detected by faculty or college health services. If so, colleges sometimes have the resources to support economic challenges, accommodation for assignments, and counseling resources. Bradley could be connected to supports either within the college or he may feel more comfortable and anonymous with community resources.

Case Study 1-2

Alex and Sydney were in a same-sex relationship. Alex was extremely jealous of Sydney when they would go out as Sydney would always get attention and invitations. Sydney's parents were not aware that they are nonbinary, and Alex was angry that Sydney had not "come out of the closet." Alex began threatening to tell Sydney's parents and consequently, Sydney would become anxious at Alex's behavior when they visited. After a night out, Alex was particularly upset and angry, and began screaming and throwing things at Sydney. Sydney told Alex they had enough and were leaving. Alex grabbed Sydney and held them down before sexually assaulting them. Immediately after, Sydney gathered their clothes and ran out the door. Sydney came to the hospital and requested a sexual assault examination, but did not want police involved. Alex then came into the hospital demanding to see Sydney.

Sydney was eventually discharged. They did not report to police and did not want referral to resources. Staff were concerned about the level of risk given the sexual assault and coercive control pattern.

Discussion

Alex was demanding to visit, but Sydney should be asked for a preference. There may be fear on Sydney's part to refuse Alex. This should be explored—if Sydney wants Alex to visit, it is their choice and part of trauma-informed care to empower choice. If Sydney does not want Alex in, the health care provider may have options, such as health care information acts or privacy policies of the institution which can be used to prevent Alex from visiting, while also protecting Sydney from retaliation when discharged.

Alex's behaviors were controlling and coercive. They were attempting to get Sydney to "come out" and threatening to do so. Unlike situational violence, this was an escalating pattern of control and emotional abuse, culminating in sexual violence. It is therefore consistent with coercive control behavior. Interpersonal violence is more prevalent in LGBTQIA+ relationships than heterosexual relationships. The person's sexuality can also be used as a means of coercive control against the partner, and there may be an absence of informal supports (eg, friends and family) as well as limited community supports. Even accessing the community supports may "out" Sydney, further isolating them.

Those experiencing interpersonal violence typically return to the relationship many times before leaving long-term. It is their choice, per trauma-informed care. If Sydney refuses the referrals, professionals should let them know about options such as safety plans and that when ready, they may want to consider taking action with these options.

Summary

Interpersonal violence affects all ages and types of relationships. Even after relationships are over, there is a risk of homicide or continued abuse. The adverse mental and physical effects can be life-changing and intergenerational. Prevention is important and requires an understanding that abuse risk factors are complex and intersectional. Accordingly, the prevention and intervention must address this complexity. The use of the social-ecological model directs screening and interventions at multiple levels. Although not universally accepted, use of Johnson's typology in future research may help identify interventions that are more effective with one type of abuse than another. Early detection through universal screening is important and also should be conducted in multiple settings and with a TIA. This may assist in moving victims from pre-contemplation levels towards seeking support and leaving the situation.

References

1. Brieding M, Basile KC, Smith SG. *Intimate Partner Violence Surveillance: Uniform Definitions and Recommended Data Elements, Version 2.0.* Centers for Disease Control and Prevention; 2015. https://stacks.cdc.gov/view/cdc/31292

2. Fact sheet: intimate partner violence. Government of Canada. 2025. https://www.canada.ca/en/women-gender-equality/gender-based-violence/intimate-partner-violence.html

3. Sexual assault and other sexual offences. Government of Canada. 2021. https://www.justice.gc.ca/eng/rp-pr/cj-jp/victim/rr14_01/p10.html

4. Pinchevsky GM, Augustyn MB, Kennedy AH, Rennison CM. Perceptions of sexual violence terms used in statutes throughout the United States. *Violence Against Women*. 2024;30(15-16):3991-4011. doi:10.1177/10778012231188088

5. Violence against women prevalence estimates, 2018. World Health Organization. 2021. https://iris.who.int/bitstream/handle/10665/341338/9789240026681-eng.pdf?sequence=1

6. Carter-Snell C. Youth dating violence: the silent epidemic. In: Taylor M, Pooley JA, Taylor RS, eds. *Overcoming Domestic Violence: Creating a Dialogue Around Vulnerable Populations*. Nova Science; 2015:49-65.

7. Basile KC, Clayton HB, DeGue S, et al. Violence victimization among high school students-youth risk behavior survey, United States, 2019. *MMWR Morb Mortal Wkly Rep*. 2020;69(1):28-37. doi:10.15585/mmwr.su6901a4

8. Casiano H, Katz LY, Globerman D, Sareen J. Suicide and deliberate self-injurious behavior in juvenile correctional facilities: a review. *J Can Acad Child Adolesc Psychiatry*. 2013;22(2):118-124.

9. Taquette SR, Maia Monteiro DL. Causes and consequences of adolescent dating violence: a systematic review. *J Inj Violence Res*. 2019;11(2):137-147. doi:10.5249/jivr.v11i2.1061

10. Smith SG, Zhang X, Basile KC, et al. *The National Intimate Partner and Sexual Violence Survey (NISVS): 2015 Data Brief*. Centers for Disease Control and Prevention. November 2018. https://stacks.cdc.gov/view/cdc/60893

11. Heim C, Nemeroff CB. Neurobiology of posttraumatic stress disorder. *CNS Spectr*. 2009;14(1):13-24.

12. Ford-Gilboe M, Varcoe C, Wuest J, et al. Trajectories of depression, post-traumatic stress, and chronic pain among women who have separated from an abusive partner: a longitudinal analysis. *J Interpers Violence*. 2023;38(1-2):NP1540-NP1568. doi:10.1177/08862605221090595

13. Carter-Snell C, Hegadoren K. Stress disorders and gender: implications for theory and research. *Can J Nurs Res*. 2003;35(2):34-55.

14. Powers RA, Kleppe A, Amory KL, Jennings WG, Cochran JK. The role of perpetrator tactics on physical and mental health outcomes associated with intimate partner sexual violence: a sex-specific analysis. *Violence Vict*. 2022;37(2):165-184. doi:10.1891/VV-D-20-00046

15. Maskin RM, Iverson KM, Vogt D, Smith BN. Associations between intimate partner violence victimization and employment outcomes among male and female post-9/11 veterans. *Psychol Trauma*. 2019;11(4):406-414. doi:10.1037/tra0000368

16. Wathen CN, MacGregor JCD, Tanaka M, MacQuarrie BJ. The impact of intimate partner violence on the health and work of gender and sexual minorities in Canada. *Int J Public Health*. 2018;63(8):945-955. doi:10.1007/s00038-018-1127-1

17. Ørke EC, Vatnar SKB, Bjørkly S. Risk for revictimization of intimate partner violence by multiple partners: a systematic review. *J Fam Violence*. 2018;33(5):325-339. doi:10.1007/s10896-018-9952-9

18. Lafontaine MF, Azzi S, Bell-Lee B, Dixon-Luinenburg T, Guérin-Marion C, Bureau JF. Romantic perfectionism and perceived conflict mediate the link between insecure romantic attachment and intimate partner violence in undergraduate students. *J Fam Violence.* 2021;36(2):195-208. doi:10.1007/s10896-020-00130-y

19. Haskell L, Randall M. *The Impact of Trauma on Adult Sexual Assault Victims.* Canada J; 2019:1-49. https://www.justice.gc.ca/eng/rp-pr/jr/trauma/trauma_eng.pdf

20. Smith PH, Tessaro I, Earp JA. Women's experiences with battering: a conceptualization from qualitative research. *Womens Health Issues.* 1995;5(4):173-182. doi:10.1016/1049-3867(95)00615-X

21. Lahav Y. Hyper-sensitivity to the perpetrator and the likelihood of returning to abusive relationships. *J Interpers Violence.* 2023;38(1-2):NP1815-NP1841. doi:10.1177/08862605221092075

22. Callaway CCM, Ch'ang JH. Traumatic brain injury in intimate partner violence. *Curr Pain Headache Rep.* 2025;29(1):6. doi:10.1007/s11916-024-01324-5

23. Khurana B, Bayne HN, Temple J, Andover P, Loder R. Comparative analysis of injuries related to self-harm, assault, and intimate partner violence: insights from the US Emergency Departments (2005-2021). *Inj Prev.* 2025. doi:10.1136/ip-2024-045435

24. Carter-Snell C. Injury documentation: Using the BALD STEP Mnemonic and the RCMP Sexual Assault Kit. *NENA Outlook.* 2011;34(1):15-20.

25. Carter-Snell CJ. *Understanding Women's Risks for Injury From Sexual Assault.* 2007. https://era.library.ualberta.ca/items/ec94bccc-1e52-4932-a35d-e88d0a62839b

26. Baker RB, Fargo JD, Shambley-Ebron D, Sommers MS. A source of health-care disparity: race, skin color, and injuries after rape among adolescents and young adults. *J Forensic Nurs.* 2010;6(3):144-150. doi:10.1111/j.1939-3938.2010.01070.x

27. Burczycka M. Section 2: police-reported intimate partner violence, 2018. *Juristat.* 2019. https://www150.statcan.gc.ca/n1/pub/85-002-x/2019001/article/00018/02-eng.htm

28. Pastor-Moreno G, Ruiz-Pérez I, Henares-Montiel J, Escribà-Agüir V, Higueras-Callejón C, Ricci-Cabello I. Intimate partner violence and perinatal health: a systematic review. *BJOG.* 2020;127(5):537-547. doi:10.1111/1471-0528.16084

29. Sinko L, Hughesdon K, Grotts JH, Giordano N, Choi KR. A systematic review of research on trauma and women's health in the nurses' health study II. *Nurs Womens Health.* 2022;26(2):116-127. doi:10.1016/j.nwh.2022.01.005

30. Gilbert LK, Zhang X, Basile KC, Breiding M, Kresnow MJ. Intimate partner violence and health conditions among US adults—National Intimate Partner Violence Survey, 2010–2012. *J Interpers Violence.* 2023;38(1-2):NP237-NP261. doi:10.1177/08862605221080147

31. Felitti VJ. The relation between adverse childhood experiences and adult health: turning gold into lead. *Perm J.* 2002;6(1):44-47. doi:10.7812/tpp/02.994

32. Gallagher AR, Moreland ML, Watters KN, Yalch MM. Relative effects of childhood trauma, intimate partner violence, and other traumatic life events on complex posttraumatic stress disorder symptoms. *Traumatology.* 2023;29(1):57-64. doi:10.1037/trm0000379

33. Krug EG, Dahlberg LL, Mercy JA, Zwi AB, Lozano R. *World Report on Violence and Health.* World Health Organization; 2002. https://iris.who.int/bitstream/handle/10665/42495/9241545615_eng.pdf

34. Yakubovich AR, Stöckl H, Murray J, et al. Risk and protective factors for intimate partner violence against women: systematic review and meta-analyses of prospective-longitudinal studies. *Am J Public Health.* 2018;108(7):e1-e11. doi:10.2105/AJPH.2018.304428

35. The social-ecological model: a framework for prevention. Centers for Disease Control and Prevention. 2009.

36. Román-Gálvez RM, Martín-Peláez S, Fernández-Félix BM, Zamora J, Khan KS, Bueno-Cavanillas A. Worldwide prevalence of intimate partner violence in pregnancy. a systematic review and meta-analysis. *Front Public Health.* 2021;9:738459. doi:10.3389/fpubh.2021.738459

37. Daigle LE, Hawk SR. Sexual orientation, revictimization, and polyvictimization. *Sex Res Social Policy.* 2022;19(1):308-320. doi:10.1007/s13178-021-00543-4

38. King KA, Yockey RA, Vidourek RA. Transgender individuals and psychological intimate partner violence: a national study. *J Fam Violence.* 2022;37(2):289-300. doi:10.1007/s10896-020-00219-4

39. Cotter A. Intimate partner violence in Canada 2018: an overview. Statistics Canada. 2021. https://www150.statcan.gc.ca/n1/en/pub/85-002-x/2021001/article/00003-eng.pdf?st=41iPLuLC

40. Lysova A, Dim EE. Severity of victimization and formal help seeking among men who experienced intimate partner violence in their ongoing relationships. *J Interpers Violence.* 2022;37(3-4):1404-1429. doi:10.1177/0886260520922352

41. Warthe DG, Carter-Snell C, Choate P. Men's experiences of dating and domestic violence on a post-secondary campus. Mount Royal University. 2022. https://www.mtroyal.ca/ProgramsCourses/FacultiesSchoolsCentres/HealthCommunityEducation/Departments/ChildStudiesandSocialWork/RelationshipViolencePrevention/mens-experiences-with-violence.htm

42. Varlioglu R, Hayes BE. Gender differences in the victim-offender overlap for dating violence: the role of early violent socialization. *Child Abuse Negl.* 2022;123:105428. doi:10.1016/j.chiabu.2021.105428

43. Adverse childhood experiences. Centers for Disease Control and Prevention. 2024. https://www.cdc.gov/aces/about/index.html44

44. Evans KE, Schmidt-Sane MM, Bender AE, Berg KA, Holmes MR. Children's exposure to intimate partner violence and acceptance or appraisals of IPV: a systematic review. *J Fam Violence.* 2022;37(5):1-19. doi:10.1007/s10896-021-00318-w

45. Simone L, Wettstein A, Senn O, Rosemann T, Hasler S. Types of abuse and risk factors associated with elder abuse. *Swiss Med Wkly.* 2016;146:w14273. doi:10.4414/smw.2016.14273

46. Ahmadabadi Z, Najman JM, Williams GM, Clavarino AM. Income, gender, and forms of intimate partner violence. *J Interpers Violence.* 2020;35(23-24):5500-5525. doi:10.1177/0886260517719541

47. Reichel D. Determinants of intimate partner violence in Europe: the role of income status, inequality, and partner behavior. *J Interpers Violence.* 2017;32(12):1853-1873. doi:10.1177/0886260517698951

48. Corbett E, Theobald J, Billett P, Hooker L, Edmonds L, Fisher C. Revictimisation of women in non-urban areas: a scoping review. *Trauma Violence Abuse.* 2023;24(4):2379-2394. doi:10.1177/15248380221094317

49. Moffitt P, Aujla W, Giesbrecht CJ, Grant I, Straatman AL. Intimate partner violence and COVID-19 in rural, remote, and northern Canada: relationship, vulnerability and risk. *J Fam Violence.* 2022;37(5):775-786. doi:10.1007/s10896-020-00212-x

50. Toccalino D, Haag HL, Estrella MJ, et al. Addressing the shadow pandemic: COVID-19 related impacts, barriers, needs, and priorities to health care and support for women survivors of intimate partner violence and brain injury. *Arch Phys Med Rehabil.* 2022;103(7):1466-1476. doi:10.1016/j.apmr.2021.12.012

51. Littleton H, Edwards KM, Sall KE, Lim S, Mauer V. COVID-Specific coercive control among emerging adults attending college: a brief note. *J Fam Violence.* 2022:1-7. doi:10.1007/s10896-022-00403-8

52. Leigh JK, Peña LD, Anurudran A, Pai A. "Are you safe to talk?": perspectives of service providers on experiences of domestic violence during the COVID-19 pandemic. *J Fam Violence.* 2022:1-11. doi:10.1007/s10896-022-00359-9

53. Smith D. Battered woman syndrome: hazards and implications. *Social Worker.* 1996;64(3):15-20.

54. Campbell JC, Webster DW, Glass N. The danger assessment: validation of a lethality risk assessment instrument for intimate partner femicide. *J Interpers Violence.* 2009;24(4):653-674. doi:10.1177/0886260508317180

55. Johnson MP, Leone JM. The differential effects of intimate terrorism and situational couple violence: findings from the National Violence Against Women Survey. *J Fam Issues.* 2005;26(3):322-349. doi:10.1177/0192513X04270345

56. Jasinski J, Blumenstein L, Morgan R. Testing Johnson's typology: is there gender symmetry in intimate terrorism? *Violence Vict.* 2014;29(1):73-88. doi:10.1891/0886-6708.VV-D-12-00146

57. Hines DA, Douglas EM. An empirical test of Johnson's typology of intimate partner violence in two samples of men. *Partner Abuse.* 2019;10(2):180-198. doi:10.1891/1946-6560.10.2.180

58. Love HA, Spencer CM, May SA, Mendez M, Stith SM. Perpetrator risk markers for intimate terrorism and situational couple violence: a meta-analysis. *Trauma Violence Abuse.* 2020;21(5):922-931. doi:10.1177/1524838018801331

59. Babcock JC, Snead AL, Bennett VE, Armenti NA. Distinguishing subtypes of mutual violence in the context of self-defense: classifying types of partner violent couples using a Modified Conflict Tactics Scale. *J Fam Violence.* 2019;34(7):687-696. doi:10.1007/s10896-018-0012-2

60. Strauss MA. Prevalence of violence against dating partners by male and female university students worldwide. *Violence Against Women.* 2004;10(7):790-811.

61. Conroy NE, Crowley CG, DeSanto DL. Assessing the state of empirical research on Johnson's typology of violence: a systematic review. *J Fam Violence.* 2024;39:23-45. doi:10.1007/s10896-022-00416-3

62. Spencer CM, Stith SM, Cafferky B. What puts individuals at risk for physical intimate partner violence perpetration? A meta-analysis examining risk markers for men and women. *Trauma Violence Abuse.* 2022;23(1):36-51. doi:10.1177/1524838020925776

63. What is Clare's Law and why is it so important to all Albertans? McGuinness Law. Accessed May 24, 2022. https://mcguinesslaw.com/article/what-is-clares-law-and-why-is-it-important-to-all-albertans/

64. Walker LEA. Psychological causes of family violence. In: Mary Lystad, ed. *Violence in the Home—Interdisciplinary Perspectives.* US Department of Justice; 1986:71-97.

65. Domestic abuse intervention programs. Updated 2024. https://www.theduluthmodel.org/

66. Zarling A, Russell D. A randomized clinical trial of acceptance and commitment therapy and the Duluth Model classes for men court-mandated to a domestic violence program. *J Consult Clin Psychol.* 2022;90(4):326-338. doi:10.1037/ccp0000722

67. Cheng SY, Wachter K, Kappas A, et al. Patterns of help-seeking strategies in response to intimate partner violence: a latent class analysis. *J Interpers Violence.* 2022;37(9-10):NP6604-NP6632. doi:10.1177/0886260520966671

68. SAMHSA's Concept of Trauma and Guidace for a Trauma-Informed Approach. Substance Abuse and Mental Health Services Administration. 2014;9-11. https://library.samhsa.gov/product/samhsas-concept-trauma-and-guidance-trauma-informed-approach/sma14-4884

69. O'Connor SA. *An Examination of The Relationship Between Peritraumatic Dissociation and Sexual Trauma.* Dissertation. Alliant International University; 2016. https://www.proquest.com/docview/1819561535

70. Campbell R. What really happened? A validation study of rape survivors' help-seeking experiences with the legal and medical systems. *Violence Vict.* 2005;20(1):55-69.

71. Thurston WE, Tutty LM, Eisener AC, Lalonde L, Belenky C, Osborne B. Implementation of universal screening for domestic violence in an urgent care community health center. *Health Promot Pract.* 2009;10(4):517-526. doi:10.1177/1524839907307994

72. Sherin KM, Sinacore JM, Ziao-Qiang L, Zitter RE, Shakil A. HITS: A short domestic violence screening tool for use in a family practice setting. *Fam Med.* 1998;30(7):508-512.

73. Feltner C, Wallace I, Berkman N, et al. Screening for intimate partner violence, elder abuse, and abuse of vulnerable adults: evidence report and systematic review for the US Preventive Services Task Force. *JAMA.* 2018;320(16):1688-1701. doi:10.1001/jama.2018.13212

74. Velonis A, Maddox R, Buhariwala P, et al. Asking the right questions: screening men for partner violence. *J Interpers Violence.* 2022;37(15-16):NP13813-NP13829. doi:10.1177/08862605211005155

75. Eulitt PJ, Tomberg RJ, Cunningham TD, Counselman FL, Palmer RM. Screening elders in the emergency department at risk for mistreatment: a pilot study. *J Elder Abuse Negl.* 2014;26(4):424-435. doi:10.1080/08946566.2014.903549

76. Fang J, Donley E. Intimate partner violence screening tools in emergency departments: a scoping review. *Practice.* 2022;34(2):149-165. doi:10.1080/09503153.2021.1959542

77. Kosiak K, Contreras IM, Stoever J, Toohey J, Novaco RW. Organization-based factors bearing on provider screening and referral practices for women exposed to intimate partner violence. *J Interpers Violence.* 2022;37(13-14):NP11520-NP11540. doi:10.1177/0886260521991894

78. Ahmad I, Ali PA, Rehman S, Talpur A, Dhingra K. Intimate partner violence screening in emergency department: a rapid review of the literature. *J Clin Nurs.* 2017;26(21-22):3271-3285. doi:10.1111/jocn.13706

79. Allen K, Melendez-Torres GJ, Ford T, et al. Family focused interventions that address parental domestic violence and abuse, mental ill-health, and substance misuse in combination: a systematic review. *PLoS One.* 2022;17(7):e0270894. doi:10.1371/journal.pone.0270894

80. DeHond A, Brady F, Kalokhe AS. Prevention of perpetration of intimate partner violence by men and boys in low- and middle-income countries: a scoping review of primary prevention interventions. *Trauma Violence Abuse.* 2023;24(4):2412-2428. doi:10.1177/15248380221097441

81. Snowdon L, Quigg Z, Leavey C. The role of public health in the primary prevention of interpersonal violence: a systematic review of international frameworks. *J Community Saf Well Being.* 2024;9(4):176-183. doi:10.35502/jcswb.406

82. Asadi N, Radi AM, Masoumi SZ, Kazemi F, Khodaveisi M. A systematic review of various interventions on domestic violence in pregnant women. *Fam Med Prim Care Rev.* 2023;25(2):197-211. doi:10.5114/fmpcr.2023.127681

83. Carter B, Paranjothy S, Davies A, Kemp A. Mediators and effect modifiers of the causal pathway between child exposure to domestic violence and internalizing behaviors among children and adolescents: a systematic literature review. *Trauma Violence Abuse.* 2022;23(2):594-604. doi:10.1177/1524838020965964

Chapter 2

A Historical Perspective: *How Have Societal Attitudes Changed Over Time, and How Far Have We Come?*

Laura Albee, MD

Objectives

After reviewing this chapter, the reader will be able to:

1. *Understand the pathways in human history that led to the propagation of domestic violence.*
2. *Understand the cultural differences that have shaped domestic violence throughout history and across the world.*
3. *Understand that domestic violence developed in patriarchal societies where women and children were regarded as property and men had a need to maintain control of society.*

Introduction

In order to understand the history of domestic violence, one must first examine the history of humanity. What is considered domestic violence today was legally and socially acceptable for thousands of years. It was not documented as domestic violence; it was a part of human life. Human societies tended to be violent, so violence at home was tolerated and not considered abnormal. It was not until the 1800s that domestic violence became recognized as a problem, much less addressed. Since the 1960s, the United States has made a great deal of progress in recognizing and combating domestic violence. Similarly, there has also been progress made in the terminology used to refer to domestic violence. As understandings of violence in the context of families and other relationships have improved, the terms used have also changed to become more inclusive. In recognizing that violence occurs in all relationship settings, not just among cohabitating heterosexual couples, domestic violence became intimate partner violence, which has since given way to gender-based violence and interpersonal violence. However, for the purposes of this chapter, which focuses on how interpersonal violence was viewed and addressed in the past, the term domestic violence will be used.

Early Humanity

Many human cultures developed as patriarchal societies. In a patriarchy, men are considered the ultimate authority and women and children are considered subjects or property. Women in early societies were granted rights only as related to their value as a man's property, while children had no rights.[1] Merriam-Webster[2] defines

Patriarchy as a "social organization marked by the supremacy of the father in the clan or family, the legal dependence of wives and children, and the reckoning of descent and inheritance in the male line." More broadly, the term is defined as the "control by men of a disproportionately large share of power."[2] In many early societies, there were no courts or laws, so men carried out the task of protecting and controlling women and children. If a woman or child was accused of a crime, they were returned home to the man of the house to determine their guilt and punishment. A man could be punished for crimes committed outside the home by a woman in his family.

Before the Common Era (BCE)

Hammurabi's Code from ancient Babylon is the oldest known written legal code, dating back to 1780 BCE.[3] During this time, women did not control their own wealth; therefore, a woman's family wealth was controlled by her father or husband. The code also contained provisions for the discipline of wives and children by their husband or father.[4] An example from Hammurabi's Code includes, "An unmarried virgin daughter who was raped by a man not already married was forced to marry her rapist. The rapist's only penalty was to marry the girl and pay her father a fine."[1] It was legal to drown a wife if she left her husband without proving his cruelty to her. If she was caught committing adultery, her husband was allowed to tie her up and drown her, possibly even tied to the man she committed adultery with.[4,5] The code also states that "If a man strikes a free-born woman so that she loses her unborn child, he shall pay ten shekels for her loss," and, "If the woman dies, his daughter shall be put to death."[5]

In the Roman Empire, the male head of the household was given the right to beat, divorce, and even murder his wife if she offended or disobeyed her husband. Husbands were also permitted to kill their wives for adultery and going outside without modest clothing. The male head of the household was allowed to decide whether a newborn baby would be raised and cared for as part of the family or if they would be abandoned to die.[4] A Roman husband possessed *patria potestas* (literally, "power of a father"), which included the power to sell his wife and children into slavery or put them to death.[6]

Early Common Era (CE) and the Middle Ages

Constantine the Great (well-known for being the emperor to establish Christianity as the official religion of Rome) was the first emperor to execute his wife, boiling her alive for suspected adultery. He also had his eldest son put to death for plotting against him and had some of his in-laws executed. He was later canonized as a saint in the Catholic Church.[1]

The level of violence in a society or time period influenced how much violence was tolerated at home. During the Roman Empire, armed combat to the death with other men or wild animals was a form of entertainment.[1] There was a high rate of crime, and public punishments in front of massive cheering crowds were standard. Plagues in Europe decimated the population, and infant mortality was common. Domestic violence was considered to be a normal form of familial interaction, and it paled in comparison to the level of violence occurring throughout society.

The Middle Ages in Europe encompasses the time period from the fall of the Roman Empire to the fall of Constantinople (ie, 476-1453). In Europe during this time, women were denied education and were not allowed to participate in politics. They were subject to arranged marriages, and the value of women was centered on housekeeping duties and breeding. This is still the case for women in many parts of the world. Additionally, women could be burned alive for nagging or having a miscarriage, and children could be abandoned, bonded for labor, or sold into slavery.

Early Modern Era

Biblical laws and moral codes considered women and children less important than men and provided them with fewer individual rights. The Catholic Church established the "Rules of Marriage" or "Rule for Married Life," written by Friar Cherubino in 1477. Men were advised to use scolding, bullying, terror, and beatings to reportedly save the woman's soul from her evil ways. A husband was proclaimed to be the judge over his wife, and beating her was recommended as an accepted form of discipline that would benefit her soul.[4]

"But if your wife is of a servile condition, rustic and ill-mannered character, that with these pleasant words she is not amended, rebuke her with harsh and sharp words, threats, and other fears. And if this is still not enough, and you see her do something offensive to God, injurious to her soul, your or her shame, or another noteworthy danger, take up the stick and beat her well; because it is better to be scourged in the body and to heal the soul than to lose the body and damn the soul."[7]

Figure 2-1

Figure 2-1. *The caption on this French illustration from 1845 reads "Qui aime bien châtie bien" or "He who loves well punishes well."*[8]

The saying "Rule of Thumb" was derived from an English common law that allowed a man to beat his wife with a stick of smaller circumference than his thumb.[1] This represented an improvement in the treatment of women by putting a limit on the level of violence a man was permitted to inflict on his wife. French laws allowed a husband to place blows of any kind on a woman's back as long as the punishment left no permanent marks (**Figure 2-1**). Men were considered to not really be men if they were not the masters of their wives.[1]

Domestic Violence in the Early United States

Colonization

In the United States, the colonies were established by immigrants from all over Europe who were attempting to make a better life for themselves. They fled poverty, religious oppression, and lack of opportunity. The Puritans were early colonists who settled in North America during the 1600s. Puritan faith was strict and required absolute obedience. They depended on a tight social order rooted in faith, to keep them secure.[4] The need to discipline sinners made it socially acceptable to physically punish wives and children. Violence in the home was permitted so long as it did not make the family's neighbors uncomfortable. The sanctity of marriage was considered extremely important in Puritan society; it was viewed as a covenant between man, woman, God, community, and church. Women were considered subordinate and were expected to follow biblical commands as well as obey and submit to men. A good Puritan woman was expected to blame herself and adjust her behavior rather than try to escape repeated punishment.[1] However, the Puritans enacted the first laws anywhere in the world against wife-beating and "unnatural severity" to children.[6] In 1641, the Puritans of the Massachusetts Bay Colony passed a law that made spousal abuse illegal, though this law was open to interpretation and provided for the use of "legitimate" force in the home.[8]

The Late Modern Period

The Temperance Movement from 1799 to 1860 promoted moderation or abstinence from alcohol. While the earliest temperance society was controlled by men, by the 1840s, women were also becoming involved and advancing the movement. This led to the creation of organizations such as the Women's Christian Temperance Union (WCTU). These organizations focused on prohibiting the sale and consumption of alcohol, as they believed that related social problems (eg, domestic violence) would subsequently disappear (**Figure 2-2**).[8] During that time, wife abuse was redefined as

Figure 2-2. *"Quarrels between Mr. and Mrs. Latimer, and brutal violence between them, were the natural consequences of the too frequent use of the bottle," reads this illustration from the temperance era.[8] Image Source: https://wellcomeimages.org/indexplus/image/V0019413.html*

harmful, but violence against single women remained acceptable. Stories from the temperance movement tell of a drunken father climbing into bed with his young daughter. This was not viewed as rape, but as his daughter's love saving him from his alcohol addiction.

Feminists during the Antebellum period (ie, 1812-1861) campaigned for liberalization of divorce laws. They believed that it was a "cruel perversion of marriage and motherhood to require a woman to remain married to a husband who was made brutish by alcohol."[8] However, some court cases in the 1800s in the United States permitted ongoing domestic violence. In 1824, the case *Bradley v State of Mississippi*[9] led to the state Supreme Court affirming a husband's right to use physical force against his wife in "cases of emergency" as long as no permanent injury occurred. In 1874, a North Carolina case, *State v Oliver,*[1] permitted violence by a husband as long as it was not due to malice or cruelty.

In 1848, the Seneca Falls Convention for women's rights was held in New York.[4] It was the first convention to discuss the social, civil, and religious conditions and rights of women. During this time, slavery was still commonplace throughout the United States, and domestic violence toward and amongst slaves was accepted. When the Emancipation Proclamation was enacted in 1863 during the Civil War, those who were previously enslaved became recognized as free individuals.[4] It took many decades before previously enslaved individuals and their families were fully recognized as citizens under the law and were given the same protections as other Americans.

When Frances Willard, the president of WCTU, died in 1898, the fight for women's issues subsided. "There was virtually no public discussion of wife beating from the turn of the century until the mid-1970s."[8] This lack of discussion had previously changed in the 1870s and 1880s when, in 1871, Alabama became the first state to rescind the legal right of men to beat their wives after a former slave, George Fulgham, was charged with assaulting his wife. The court ruled that "a married woman is as much under the protection of the law as any other member of the community."[4] This case represented a turning point in perceptions towards domestic violence, and it was the beginning of a nationwide movement against domestic violence.[4] Later, in 1882, Maryland became the first state to make wife-beating a crime, punishable by 40 lashes or a year in jail.[8,9]

Violence in Native American Communities

Native Americans deserve separate consideration when studying domestic violence in North America. Native American women experienced rapid social change as European colonization occurred, including decimation by European diseases, Christian missionizing, and forced relocation to less desirable geographic areas or boarding schools. Within Navajo culture, women traditionally shared equal rights with men, and they sometimes enjoyed superior authority and importance. Before 1833, marriage practices, divorce, and inheritance were strongholds of women's power within the tribe.[10] Divorce could be enacted by a woman simply by removing her husband's belongings from the home. In 1886, the United States federal government passed the Dawes Act, which required the allotment of Native lands to be made to men, not women.[10] United States government leaders insisted that the Navajos select male leaders. Until then, Navajo women had held a strong role in the public decisions of Navajo clan groups. From 1850 to 1950, the federal government practiced widespread systematic removal of Native children from their families and communities. The children were placed into state- and church-run boarding schools. These boarding schools were a traumatic experience for many children, who suffered physical, sexual, and emotional abuse.[10] Native Americans were forced into patriarchy and poverty, and today they still suffer the effects of having their communities and cultures uprooted. Native American reservations currently exist on large expanses of less desirable land with poor infrastructure, poverty, and limited law enforcement, among other issues. This makes it more difficult for women on reservations to seek help and escape an abusive situation.

On some reservations and in certain counties in the United States, Native American women are murdered and sexually assaulted at rates 10 times the national average, which has led to the coining of the term Missing and Murdered Indigenous Women (MMIW).[11,12] Nationwide, Native American women are 2 times more likely to experience rape or sexual assault, and from 1999 to 2019, homicide was the third leading cause of death among American Indian and Alaska Native women.[11,12] These crimes typically occur in remote settings where transient workers in oil fields, mining, and logging live in temporary housing units called "man camps" on and near Indigenous people's lands.[12] Many of these remote reservations lack even a single police officer, and where officers do exist, there is confusion between Indigenous, local, and state police jurisdictions, causing investigations into missing Indigenous women to be delayed or never occur.[13] Accurate data on crimes against Native Americans is difficult to obtain due to the fact that many crime databases do not include crime reports from Native American nations.[12] "Indigenous women [are] subjected to a version of justice that is completely different from everybody else," according to Rachel Ward, research director for Amnesty International USA.[11]

Some states started making efforts in 2019 to address the MMIW crisis by launching task forces or committees. Advocates believe that more effort is needed at the national level to address this complex issue. The 1994 Violence Against Women Act (VAWA) largely failed to protect Native American women, however, it was reauthorized in 2013 to give Native American nations jurisdiction over domestic violence cases committed against Native Americans on their lands.[12] This included the crimes of domestic violence, dating violence, and criminal violations of a qualifying protection order. In 2019, a 2-year Presidential Task Force on Missing and Murdered American Indians and Alaska Natives, also known as Operation Lady Justice, was launched.[11] Interior Secretary Deb Haaland is the first Native American Cabinet Secretary in United States' history, and in 2021, she announced the formation of a new Missing and Murdered Unit within the Bureau of Indian Affairs.[11] VAWA 2022 was signed in March 2022 by President Biden. It builds on VAWA 2013 by adding recognition of a nation's inherent criminal justice system over non-Natives' for: child violence, sexual violence, stalking, sex trafficking, assaults of Indigenous justice personnel, and obstruction of justice.[14] It went into effect on October 1, 2022.

Discrimination in Domestic Violence Cases

From the 1600s through the 1900s in North America, there was variation in how family violence was viewed. There were times when protecting the family unit was expected and alternating periods in which family violence was recognized as a societal issue. A key element of reform included naming the problem, such as classifying certain types of violence as "crimes against women" and "battered child syndrome." The term battered child syndrome was introduced in 1962 in an article in the Journal of the American Medical Association (JAMA).[6] The term "crimes against women" is now referred to as violence against women and gender-based violence. Periods of inattention to domestic violence correlated with ministers, writers, and judges promoting a return to private family life and the concept of "the family ideal." Conversely, periods of progress correlated with ministers, millionaires, physicians, and activists making family violence a social issue.[6]

In the United States, there were often differences in court rulings based on race and economic class. Rulings involving middle- to upper-class White men focused on family privacy and preserving the family unit. Lower class men, including Black men, were more likely to be found guilty of "gross abuse." If a woman left an abusive spouse during the 1800s and 1900s, her children would likely end up in an orphanage or foster care if she was unable to find work. Alimony orders were not enforceable, so divorced, battered women could end up living on public charity.[6]

Legal Advances for Battered Women

In 1911, the first family court was created in Buffalo, New York, as an attempt to resolve family problems in a setting for discussion and reconciliation with social services rather than punishment through the criminal court system.[9] In 1962, New York domestic violence cases were transferred to a family court rather than a civil court. However, a man would still face harsher penalties for assaulting a stranger than for assaulting his wife.[15] 1918 to 1939 was a period of massive change for battered women in the United States. In 1919, the 19th amendment was passed, giving women the right to vote. For the first time in United States' history, women were able to have a say in the laws that governed them. Additionally, there was an increase in employment options for women during this time due to men leaving for war, and divorces were also granted more frequently.

The Women's Liberation Movement

The 1960s and 1970s were transformational times in the United States regarding women's rights. This period of time brought more social liberalism involving abortion and contraception rights, gay liberation, and the legalization of interracial marriage. As a result of increased public awareness, the 1960s brought an increase in reports of child abuse and domestic violence. In 1962, JAMA published an article by Kempe et al[16] about battered child syndrome. The authors reported the first epidemiologic study and highlighted important aspects of the evaluation of suspected abuse.

Since then, several developments have occurred regarding maltreatment of children in the United States, including:

> "the establishment of county- or state-based child protective services (CPS) agencies, which are responsible for the investigation of suspected maltreatment, decisions about whether a child has been maltreated, placement of children in foster care when necessary, and services for the families when maltreatment has occurred; the broadening of the term 'child abuse' to 'child maltreatment,' which now includes physical abuse, neglect, sexual abuse, and emotional maltreatment; and the establishment in 2009 of a new pediatrics subspecialty, child abuse pediatrics."[17]

In 1965, Congress began passing laws that prohibited discrimination against women in employment and required equal pay for equal work.[15] In 1966, beating a spouse became grounds for divorce, but the plaintiff had to prove that a sufficient number of beatings had taken place.[9] In 1967, the state of Maine opened one of the first shelters for women in the United States. In 1969, California adopted a no-fault divorce law by which either partner can request and obtain a divorce without fear of being contested by the other partner.[15] The Women's Liberation Movement continued through the 1970s, claiming that family violence was a political issue,[9] and it set the stage for the Battered Women's Movement. Following this, hotlines and crisis centers were created to help women speak out about abuse and find help.[15]

Feminists began to speak more publicly about violence targeted at women, including spousal abuse and sexual assault. The mantra of the movement against domestic violence was "We will not be beaten!"[9] During this movement, 3 major contributing factors to violence against women were recognized: traditional gender role expectations, economic disparity, and a criminal justice system that did not hold men accountable for committing violence against women.[9] Feminists argued that rape, domestic violence, sexual harassment, and all other kinds of sexual violence were not a natural part of family life. These behaviors resulted from an abuse of power rather than from the gratification of sexual needs.[8]

Informational networks between women began sharing information, strategies, and support. By 1975, most states allowed wives to bring criminal action against their husbands for inflicting physical injury. In 1976, the International Tribunal on Crimes Against Women met in Belgium. They lit candles and took to the streets to denounce violence against women. In 1977, "Take Back the Night" was used at an anti-violence rally in Pittsburgh. San Francisco held a Take Back the Night demonstration in 1978 (**Figure 2-3**). They began to gain confidence and strength for their cause and turned fear into mass anger.[9] Take Back the Night is now an annual event, observed throughout the United States as well as internationally, that brings community members together to speak out about sexual violence, relationship violence, and other forms of interpersonal violence. Thousands of Take Back the Night marches and rallies have taken place worldwide, including on college campuses, and this tradition continues (**Figure 2-4**).

Throughout the 1970s, programs were developed across the United States to provide funding and support for battered women and victims of domestic violence, as women who left their husbands could be denied welfare based on their husband's salaries.[15]

Figure 2-3. *San Francisco, 1978; Photo by Suzanne Lacy, credit to takebackthenight.org for the use of this photo.*

Figure 2-4. *Boston, MA, 1979; Photo by Spencer Grant, credit to takebackthenight.org for the use of this photo.*

States also began to consider domestic violence a punishable crime rather than a civil matter suited for family court.

In 1981, the first Domestic Violence Awareness Week was celebrated.[15] By 1983, over 700 shelters were in operation nationwide, serving 91 000 women and 131 000 children per year. By 1989, there were 1200 battered women programs that sheltered around 300 000 women and children per year.[9] In 1984, New York's highest court made marital rape a crime, striking down the "marital rape exemption" in the case of *People v Liberta.*[15] Throughout the 1980s, programs were started in New York to combat violence against immigrant women.[15]

The 1990s Through Today

During the 1990s in the United States, legal progress continued regarding matters of domestic violence. Stalking was identified as a crime in 1990, and for the first time, judges were required to consider any history of spousal abuse before determining child custody and visitation rights. 48 states had injunctions in place to refrain men from harassing, abusing, and assaulting the women with whom they live. Emergency protection orders could be obtained outside of normal court hours in 23 states. In 1991, 1 out of 7 wives reported being raped by their husband.[15] In 1992, abuse by husbands was the leading cause of injuries to women ages 15 to 44.[9] That same year, the American Medical Association released guidelines suggesting that doctors screen women for signs of domestic violence. Then, in 1993, the United Nations recognized domestic violence as an international human rights issue and issued the Declaration on the Elimination of Violence Against Women. It was the first international instrument explicitly addressing violence against women and provided a framework for national and international action.[18] In 1996, California passed a bill to protect children from the effects of domestic abuse by giving the court the authority to remove the battering parent from the home and allowed the nonoffending parent to create a safety plan to protect the child.[9]

In 1994, the Family Protection and Domestic Violence Intervention Act brought about the development of the Order of Protection Registry and Domestic Incidence Reporting System. The federal VAWA in 1994 created legislation acknowledging domestic violence and sexual assault as crimes. It became the first federal effort to define domestic violence as a violation of a victim's civil rights. Women in both

Figure 2-5. *The Houston Area Women's Center, established in 1977, was and is dedicated to assisting victims of sexual and domestic violence.*[8]

houses of Congress became major sponsors of legislation that focused on rape and battered women. President Joseph Biden, a Democratic senator at the time, gained the support of Republican Orrin Hatch on the Senate Judiciary Committee.[15] The VAWA was passed by framing it as a law-and-order issue, and it provided additional funding for battered women's shelters (**Figure 2-5**), more prosecutors, police and judges, and the training of hospital personnel.[15] During the 1990s, all states criminalized marital rape.

International Perspective

Just as the Women's Rights Movement expanded in the United States, other nations began establishing formal laws that limited or prohibited domestic violence. In 1975, a man in Scotland was fined for hitting his wife in the face, after which the Magistrate stated that he could strike his wife on the bottom but not on the face.[9] During the same year, Brazil passed a penal code that prohibited husbands from selling, renting, or gambling away their wives.[9] In 1976, over 8000 women from 33 countries met in Brussels for the International Tribunal on Crimes Against Women. The conference covered issues involving rape, battering, forced sterilization, and mutilation, as well as economic and legal crimes against women.[15] In 1979, the General Assembly of the United Nations adopted the Convention on the Elimination of All Forms of Discrimination Against Women (CEDAW), often referred to as the "international bill of women's human rights."[19] By accepting the Convention, countries commit themselves to undertake a series of measures to end discrimination against women in all forms, including[20]:

— To incorporate the principle of equality of men and women in their legal system, abolish all discriminatory laws, and adopt appropriate laws prohibiting discrimination against women

— To establish tribunals and other public institutions to ensure the effective protection of women from discrimination

— To ensure the elimination of all acts of discrimination against women by persons, organizations, or enterprises

By 2014, CEDAW had been ratified by 187 United Nations member states. The states that had not yet ratified it at the time included South Sudan, Iran, and the

United States.[19] As of March 2022, the United States has ratified 5 of 18 International Human Rights Treaties developed by CEDAW.[21]

While there are many international movements to reduce domestic violence globally, there are still many nations where violence against women is commonplace. Examples of various practices that enable domestic violence are outlined in **Table 2-1**.

Table 2-1. Examples of Various Practices that Enable Domestic Violence

Practice	About
Female Infanticide	— Most frequently practiced in India — Practiced to prevent a loss of family money through a dowry or other expenses[19] — Estimates suggest that "among the stock of women that could potentially be alive in India today, over 25 million are missing"[22]
Female Genital Mutilation (FGM)	— Common practice in 26 African nations — 80% of all cases are in Africa with more than 200 million females affected worldwide[23] — FGM leads to higher rates of maternal mortality and neonatal death
Early and Enforced Marriage	— Common occurrence throughout Africa, Asia, and the Middle East — Niger has the highest prevalence of child marriage in the world with 75% of all girls under 18 and 33% of girls under age 15 being married[19] — Young brides often contract HIV from their much older husbands[19] — "Child, early, and forced marriage is a confluence of the multiple violations of the rights of girls. It is about poverty, discrimination and exclusion; it is violence against women and girls, abuse, rape, and exploitation. Forced marriage is abduction. It is illegal, immoral, and an unacceptable harmful practice."[19]
Honor Killings	— Most frequently practiced in Pakistan — The victims tend to be young women and the killings are often carried out by multiple family members in collaboration — In most cases, the distinction between a woman being guilty of sexual impropriety and a woman being alleged to be guilty is irrelevant as the man's honor is of utmost importance to society[19] — Most revolve around a person acting too western or wanting to adopt the culture where they live rather than follow the culture and rules of their family

Summary

Tremendous progress has been made throughout the United States and other countries to decrease the incidence of domestic violence and increase legal punishment to those who commit acts of domestic violence. However, gender-based violence and interpersonal violence are still common throughout the United States and across the globe, including rape, wife-beating, human trafficking, prostitution, stalking, honor killing, infanticide, feticide, forced child marriage, FGM, and other forms of violence. More direction is needed at the national level to enforce the punishment of these crimes. More support is needed at the community level to provide support to victims and survivors and prosecute the offenders. More women are needed in positions of power and influence to shift the patriarchy and make the safety of women and children a priority for everyone.

References

1. Worldwide history of domestic violence. IResearchNet. https://criminal-justice.iresearchnet.com/types-of-crime/domestic-violence/worldwide-history-of-domestic-violence
2. Patriarchy. Merriam-Webster Dictionary. https://www.merriam-webster.com/dictionary/patriarchy
3. King LW. The code of hammurabi. Lillian Goldman Law Library. 2008. https://avalon.law.yale.edu/ancient/hamframe.asp
4. Fisher S. A history of domestic violence: how much have things changed? Better Help. Updated June 16, 2022. https://www.betterhelp.com/advice/domestic-violence/a-history-of-domestic-violence-how-much-have-things-changed/
5. Dunbar G. Codifying discrimination: the status of women, slaves, and freedmen in the ancient near east. *Armstrong Undergrad J Hist.* 2018;8(1):7. doi:10.20429/aujh.2018.080107
6. Pleck E. *Domestic Tyranny: The Making of American Social Policy against Family Violence from Colonial Times to the Present.* 2nd ed. University of Illinois Press; 2004.
7. Cherubino da Siena, O.F.M. *Rules of Married Life.* Translated from 15th century Italian by Caterino Tommaso, T.O.P. 2020.
8. Solic P. Private matter or public crisis? Defining and responding to domestic violence. Osu.edu. May 2015. https://origins.osu.edu/article/private-matter-or-public-crisis-defining-and-responding-domestic-violence
9. Domestic violence timeline. The Pennsylvania Child Welfare Resource Center. http://www.pacwrc.pitt.edu/Curriculum/310DomesticViolenceIssuesAnIntroductionforChildWelfareProfessionals/Handouts/HO3DomesticViolenceTimeline.pdf
10. McEachern D, VanWinkle M, Steiner S. Domestic violence among the Navajo: a legacy of colonization. *J Poverty.* 2008;2(4):31-46. doi:10.1300/J134v02n04_03
11. Haynie D. How states are addressing violence against indigenous women. US News and World Report. November 1, 2021. https://www.usnews.com/news/best-states/articles/2021-11-01/how-states-are-addressing-the-missing-indigenous-women-crisis
12. Smith-Morris C. Addressing the epidemic of missing & murdered indigenous women and girls. Cultural Survival. March 6, 2020. https://www.culturalsurvival.org/news/addressing-epidemic-missing-murdered-indigenous-women-and-girls
13. #MMIW: Missing and Murdered Indigenous Women. Sicangu Community Development Organization. November 12, 2020. https://sicangucdc.org/blog/f/mmiw-missing-and-murdered-indigenous-women?gclid=CjwKCAjwquWVBhBrEiwAt1KmwiU_6Ygg5i-saMJVDd9-vdwjnhkAbNaxzXUpqzgVD320LM710RRwghoC9bAQAvD_BwE
14. Violence Against Women Act Reauthorization Act of 2022, S 3623, 117th Cong, 2nd Sess (2022). https://www.congress.gov/bill/117th-congress/senate-bill/3623

15. Burke W. Historical roots of domestic violence. Silo.Tips. June 21, 2017. https://silo.tips/download/historical-roots-of-domestic-violence

16. Kempe CH, Silverman FN, Steele BF, Droegemueller W, Silver HK. The battered-child syndrome. *JAMA.* 1962;181(1):17-24. doi:10.1001/jama.1962.03050270019004

17. Leventhal JM, Krugman RD. "The Battered-Child Syndrome" 50 years later: much accomplished, much left to do. *JAMA.* 2012;308(1):35-36.

18. Global norms and standards: ending violence against women. UN Women. https://www.unwomen.org/en/what-we-do/ending-violence-against-women/global-norms-and-standards

19. Storkey E. *Scars Across Humanity: Understanding and Overcoming Violence Against Women.* SPCK Publishing; 2015.

20. Convention on the elimination of all forms of discrimination against women. United Nations Entity for Gender Equality and the Empowerment of Women. Updated 2007. https://www.un.org/womenwatch/daw/cedaw/

21. Ratification of 18 international human rights treaties. United Nations Human Rights Office of the High Commissioner. Updated August 2, 2020. https://indicators.ohchr.org/

22. Anderson S, Ray D. The age distribution of missing women in India. *Econ Polit Wkly.* 2012;47(47/48):87-95.

23. Eighty per cent of FGM cases happen in Africa. Federal Department of Foreign Affairs. June 2, 2021. https://www.eda.admin.ch/deza/en/home/sdc/aktuell/newsuebersicht/2021/02/engagement-gegen-genitalverstuemmelung.html

Chapter 3

Risk Factors for Experiencing Interpersonal Violence

Jen Tran, MSN, RN, SANE-A
Laura Albee, MD

Objectives

After reviewing this chapter, the reader will be able to:

1. *Become aware of risk factors that predispose a person to becoming a victim or perpetrator of interpersonal violence.*
2. *Understand childhood influences that predispose a person to relationships that involve interpersonal violence later in life, including parenting styles, adverse childhood events, schema, and coping mechanisms.*
3. *Know more about personality traits and behavioral risk factors that make a person more vulnerable to interpersonal violence.*
4. *Identify ways to build trust with and provide support to people who are experiencing interpersonal violence.*

Introduction

Risk factors for interpersonal violence have been studied extensively, with studies looking both at risk factors for perpetrating interpersonal violence and becoming a victim of interpersonal violence. There is considerable overlap in risk factors for perpetration and victimization. Most studies have focused on heterosexual couples. There are fewer studies focused on same-sex couples but this area of research is emerging, which will be touched on later in the chapter. Many of the risk factors identified for interpersonal violence may seem obvious, but it is important to document and verify these risk factors so that care providers can provide support to those at higher risk. Understanding risk factors for interpersonal violence gives a framework for how to use community services and resources to mitigate a person's risk for interpersonal violence and help people free themselves from violent or unhealthy relationships.

It is helpful to clarify some definitions before discussing risk factors for interpersonal violence. According to the World Health Organization, "Intimate partner violence refers to behavior within an intimate relationship that causes physical, sexual or psychological harm, including acts of physical aggression, sexual coercion, psychological abuse and controlling behaviors. This definition covers violence by both current and former spouses and partners."[1] This publication will use the term ***interpersonal violence*** to encompass former terminology including domestic violence and intimate partner violence (IPV). Physical abuse includes hair pulling, slapping or hitting, pushing, burning, strangulation, etc. Psychological violence includes scolding, abusive language, bullying, belittling, and financial and emotional control tactics.[2]

Identifying Risk Factors

The Centers for Disease Control and Prevention (CDC) published guidelines for risk and protective factors for experiencing and perpetrating violence.[3] This article provides an extensive list of risk factors that contribute to a person becoming a perpetrator of interpersonal violence. It also lists a few protective factors that can prevent a person from becoming a perpetrator. The National Institutes of Health (NIH) published "A Systematic Review of Risk Factors for Intimate Partner Violence."[4] This is a more comprehensive analysis of risk factors based on a review of over 200 articles. This publication uses the dynamic developmental systems perspective to organize risk factors for interpersonal violence into a conceptual framework. The risk factors described are organized into 3 categories: contextual characteristics, developmental characteristics, and relationship influences. Findings from this review article are summarized in **Table 3-1**.

Organizing risk factors into this framework helps to identify modifiable risk factors for potential intervention. Risk factors identified under developmental characteristics and relationship influences could be modified by counseling services and community programs. It also helps care providers to be aware of risk factors that are not amenable to modification like age, gender, race, and ethnicity. Being aware of risks in these groups can help professionals to recognize interpersonal violence more readily in vulnerable populations.

Statistically, women between the ages of 18 and 24 are most commonly abused.[5] Within this age range, there is a higher incidence of unplanned pregnancy, lower education levels, and unmarried status, all of which are risk factors themselves.[6] As women age, their risk for interpersonal violence declines. This is contrary to earlier views that interpersonal violence was related to a couple being trapped in marriage.[4] Pregnancy is a vulnerable time for a woman. Unplanned or mistimed pregnancy increases the risk of interpersonal violence. Interpersonal violence during pregnancy impacts the mother and the child. The mother may experience both physical injury and mental health impacts. She is at increased risk for preterm labor, low infant birth weight, and having an infant who is small for gestational age.[7,8] There is even increased risk for maternal and fetal death.[8]

Regarding gender, it is important to remember that there are similar rates of interpersonal violence perpetration and victimization affecting both males and females. Women are more likely to require medical care for physical injuries.[4] Same-sex couples have similar risk factors to heterosexual couples for experiencing interpersonal violence. Interpersonal violence in same-sex couples has not been studied as much, but studies thus far suggest that interpersonal violence in same-sex couples occurs at rates similar to or even higher than heterosexual couples.[9-11] Same-sex couples face more barriers to leaving the relationship due to lack of legal recognition of same-sex relationships, failure of law enforcement to identify violence between same-sex couples as interpersonal violence, and fewer resources available to same-sex couples.[9]

Socioeconomic factors play a role in interpersonal violence. Having parents with less than a high school education was found to be a risk factor.[6] Low verbal IQ in men is a risk factor for perpetration of interpersonal violence.[4] Unemployment and low income are relatively strong predictors of interpersonal violence across ethnic groups.[4] These factors contribute to stress, which can lead to increased rates of interpersonal violence.

When examining race, ethnicity, and acculturation, it has been shown that being a member of a minority group is a risk factor for interpersonal violence. This is most consistent for Black American couples.[4] Hispanic, Indigenous American, and Alaska Natives have also been identified as having higher incidence of interpersonal violence.[12] For Mexican and Puerto Rican American husbands, being born in the United

States was a significant risk factor for perpetration of interpersonal violence. Third generation Hispanic American husbands were even more likely to assault their wives.[4] When controlled for couples who are older, married, and have higher income, race was no longer a risk factor.[12] Stress and isolation related to minority status and acculturation may leave people without a sense of community and support.

Table 3-1. Dynamic Developmental Systems Perspective[4]

Contextual Characteristics	Developmental Characteristics	Relationship Influences
Age: In adulthood, older age is protective against victimization.	Family factors: Witnessing interpersonal violence as a child, child abuse, harsh physical discipline, and family conflict are risk factors for perpetration and victimization later in life. Parental monitoring is protective (ie, positive involvement in adolescent life and encouraging nonviolent behavior).	Relationship status: Cohabiting couples are at higher risk for interpersonal violence than married couples. Women who are single, divorced, separated, or widowed are 10 times more likely to experience interpersonal violence.
Gender: Men and women are equally likely to perpetrate interpersonal violence, but women are more likely to need medical treatment.	Peer associations: Deviant peers and having friends who perpetrate violence are risk factors for perpetration. Bully victims are at higher risk of becoming a victim of dating violence.	Relationship satisfaction: Relationship discord and low relationship satisfaction are risk factors for interpersonal violence.
Socioeconomic: Unemployment and low income are risk factors for perpetration. Neighborhood/community: Neighborhood disorder can increase an adolescent's risk of interpersonal violence. Higher levels of collective efficacy can reduce dating violence for males.	Psychological/behavioral: Early problem behaviors (eg, conduct disorder) and antisocial behavior are risk factors for perpetration. Female depression and low self-esteem increases risk for female-to-male interpersonal violence. Suicide attempts predict higher risk of injuring a partner. Emotional abuse is a risk factor for physical violence. Alcohol abuse and illegal substance use are risk factors for perpetration and victimization.	Attachment: Avoidant attachment style is a risk factor for interpersonal violence. Men with low anxiety of abandonment and poor anger control are at higher risk to perpetrate violence. Men with strong commitment to family and work have mediated effects after witnessing interpersonal violence as a child. Stronger bonding to parents is protective against becoming a victim of interpersonal violence.
Race/ethnicity: Being a member of a minority group is a risk factor for interpersonal violence. Acculturation: Being born in the United States is a significant risk factor for Mexican and Puerto Rican husbands to perpetrate interpersonal violence.	Cognitive factors: Low verbal IQ is a risk factor for perpetration of male-to-female interpersonal violence.	Negative emotionality and jealousy: A man's jealousy increases the risk of male-to-female interpersonal violence. Negative emotionality is related to perpetration of interpersonal violence and crime.

Stress levels and school context factors were mentioned but not enough research was available to make conclusions, so they were not included in this table.

Childhood Experiences as Risk Factors

The vulnerabilities for experiencing interpersonal violence start in infancy. There is considerable overlap in risk factors for perpetrators of abuse and those they abuse.

The environment in which people are raised provides the foundation for relationships as they grow up. Parents demonstrate how to treat one's family unit as well as the world at large. Poor parenting skills and modeling unhealthy relationships contribute to higher risk of being involved in interpersonal violence later in life. There are 4 parenting styles that are described throughout psychology literature: Authoritative, Authoritarian, Permissive, and Neglectful.[13] **Table 3-2** describes and compares these parenting styles.

Table 3-2. Parenting Styles

Authoritative	Authoritarian	Permissive	Neglectful
High expectations	High expectations	Low expectations	No expectations
Assertive, responsive, democratic	Autocratic, parent-driven	Child-driven	Uninvolved, passive
Warm, flexible	Forceful, rigid	Accepting, warm, lenient	Uninterested, absent
Sets clear rules, standards, and expectations	Sets strict, clear rules and punishments	Rarely gives or enforces rules	Few rules
Open communications and natural consequences	One-way communication	Overindulges child to avoid conflict	Indifferent to child's social-emotional and behavioral needs
Solves problems together with child when appropriate "Let's discuss this"	"Because I said so"	"Whatever you want"	Provides little nurturance or guidance "I don't care" "You're on your own"

Counseling services could be directed to help parents learn healthier and more effective parenting strategies. These services could be developed or presented by preschools, schools, faith organizations, and other youth community organizations. Employers could offer parenting strategy courses as part of their maternity/paternity or mental health benefits.

Adverse Childhood Experience (ACE)[14] scores are utilized in many pediatricians' offices to assess children's risk for adverse outcomes. In general, children are presented with yes or no questions regarding abuse, neglect, and other adverse experiences. Higher ACE scores predict higher incidence of medical and emotional problems as an adult.[15] ACEs increase the risk of children repeating the unhealthy behaviors and poor coping strategies of their parents (eg, alcoholism, drug use, smoking, obesity, chronic depression, and even suicide attempts).[14] ACEs could also have physiological changes that result in diseases like ischemic heart disease, liver disease, chronic lung disease, and cancer.[16]

Table 3-3. Adverse Childhood Experiences as Risk Factors[14]

Adverse Childhood Experiences	Examples
Emotional abuse	Parents who insult, humiliate, induce fear
Physical abuse	Parents who push, grab, slap, throw objects
Sexual abuse	Parents or adults who touch inappropriately, fondle, or attempt sexual activity
Emotional neglect	Children feel unloved, unimportant, or have an unsupportive family

(continued)

Table 3-3. Adverse Childhood Experiences as Risk Factors[14] *(continued)*

Adverse Childhood Experiences	Examples
Physical neglect	Children do not have enough to eat, lack clean clothes that fit well, lack medical care
Parental separation or divorce	Parental abandonment or loss of access to a parent
Parental violence	Children who witness physical abuse between parents
Substance abuse	Parents or adults who abuse alcohol or substances in the household
Mental illness	Mental illness or suicide attempt in the household
Criminal behavior	A household member who has been to prison

The Schema Therapy Model was developed by Jeffrey Young[17] as an integrative psychotherapy approach. Schemas are defined as "broad, pervasive themes regarding oneself and one's relationship with others, developed during childhood and elaborated throughout one's lifetime, and dysfunctional to a significant degree."[17] The Schema Therapy Model describes 18 early maladaptive schemas that are organized into 5 Schema Domains. (see **Table 3-4**).

Table 3-4. Schema Therapy Model[17]

5 Schema Domains	18 Early Maladaptive Schemas
Disconnection & Rejection	— Abandonment/instability — Mistrust/abuse — Emotional deprivation — Defectiveness/shame — Social isolation
Impaired Autonomy & Performance	— Dependence/incompetence — Vulnerability to harm or illness — Enmeshment/undeveloped self — Failure
Impaired Limits	— Entitlement/grandiosity — Insufficient self-control/self-dicipline
Other-Directedness	— Subjugation — Self-sacrifice — Approval-seeking/recognition-seeking
Over-Vigilance & Inhibition	— Negativity/pessimism — Emotional inhibition — Unrelenting standards/hypercriticalness — Punitiveness

In a study by Taşkale & Soygüt,[18] the authors use the Schema Therapy Model to assess differences between women residing in a domestic violence shelter and married women who had not been victims of IPV. The authors concluded that female victims of intimate partner violence are most likely to be young, have low income, and have experienced dysfunctional parenting styles as children. The schema domains, which include disconnection and unrelenting standards, were found to be predictive of IPV victimization above and beyond demographic variables and parenting styles.[18] Another study found that the domains of disconnection and rejection and impaired limits are significant predictors of becoming a victim of interpersonal violence.[19] The Schema Therapy Model provides a framework for understanding maladaptive behaviors and coping mechanisms so that therapy can be directed to help a person learn healthier patterns of behavior and thinking.

Psychological and behavioral risks include early problem behaviors like conduct disorder and antisocial behavior.[4] Female depression and low self-esteem are risk factors for females to perpetrate interpersonal violence.[4] Suicide attempts predict an increased risk of injuring a partner.[4] Alcohol abuse, binge drinking, marijuana use, and other illegal substance use are risk factors for perpetration and victimization.[4,6] Antisocial behavior and substance use problems appear to mediate most other risk factors. Substance abuse can impact a family's employment status and financial stability. Substance abuse is a poor coping mechanism that can exacerbate personality factors like antisocial behavior, depression, and violent tendencies.

Building Protection Against Interpersonal Violence

As mentioned above, there are numerous risk factors for becoming a perpetrator or victim of interpersonal violence. However, there are protective factors that have been identified that can help to reduce the effects of domestic violence on adult and child survivors. These variables are grouped in 5 categories and help provide a framework for supporting people who have experienced interpersonal violence.[15,20]

The first category is concrete support for families in times of need to create safer and more stable conditions. Families may need assistance with housing and economic stability. Provide a referral to a housing advocate who can help place a person or family into safe housing. Identify a safe method and time for communication with the victim/survivor. Include supportive family and friends in a safety plan. Provide a list of free community resources with contact information to help with immediate needs. This can include resources to help with employment, groceries, transportation and car repairs, legal issues, health care, childcare, and education. Advocate with childcare centers and schools to help maintain stability and consistency in the youth's environment. A family's needs will evolve over time, so it is important to have ongoing discussions with patients about what is working and what needs to be modified.[20]

The second category is social, cultural, and spiritual connections. Survivors are often isolated from friends and family by their abusers and do not have a feeling of connectedness. Help patients identify a social support system, which can include family, friends, neighbors, spiritual communities, cultural organizations, and family support groups. Introducing a patient to agency representatives is encouraged to help bolster feelings of connection. It is less intimidating for a survivor to follow up with someone they have met. Building trust and having honest and transparent communication is important. The Children's Bureau Learning & Coordination Center suggests to "Be authentic, compassionate and respectful to build your own relationship with adult and child survivors."[20] Help the survivor lay out reasonable goals and expectations for their life going forward. Giving the victim/survivor time to process their situation and allowing them to accept help when they are ready is essential. Forcing them to accept help can hinder building trust. Building a supportive community can improve a person's feelings of self-worth and value.

The third category is parental resilience and growth mindset. Developing a growth mindset is possible by making small, consistent changes and building on these changes over time. This is a process of personal growth and positive adaptation that involves improving coping skills, problem solving, becoming more resourceful, and functioning well in response to adversity. Therapists and support personnel can provide guidance on steps to change patterns of thinking or behavior. Once a change in thinking or behavior becomes a consistent habit, another small change can be addressed. Medical providers and mental health therapists can help patients identify and focus on their strengths, help them set goals for moving forward, and provide guidance in how to manage stress and anxiety.[20]

The fourth category is nurturing parent-child interactions. Provide education on parenting skills and child development to help parents and their children build bonds of trust, love, affection, and predictability. This helps create a sense of security in children and strengthens the parents' belief in their ability to care for and raise their children.[20] This also sets the stage for young children to learn to form healthy relationships and helps them feel confident and significant. It creates a safe and predictable environment where the child is not fearful of their parent or caregiver having irrational or unpredictable reactions to the child's behavior. Having even 1 parent or caregiver who provides nurturing interactions can be a significant positive influence, helping the child learn healthy coping skills and positive relationship and societal interactions.

The fifth category is social and emotional competence. Help survivors build stronger social and emotional abilities so they are more confident to navigate life challenges and feel more comfortable making responsible decisions.[20] This includes behavior regulation and expressing emotions in a constructive way. This is achieved through making connections, communication, de-escalation and calming strategies, setting boundaries and expectations, and including survivors in their therapy plans. Provide resources to help survivors work on problem-solving skills, help patients identify priorities, and make individual and family goals. It is important to respect a person's autonomy and ability to make decisions for themself to help bolster self-confidence and esteem.

Case Studies

Case Study 3-1

Claire was a 32-year-old woman presenting to the emergency department (ED) by ambulance from her home. She stated that she and her husband of 2 years got into an argument and it became physical. She had obvious redness and bruising to her head and was guarding her abdomen. Upon further assessment, Claire disclosed that she had been with her significant other for more than 10 years but saw a lot of "red flags," which is why it took her so long to marry him. She recently found out that she was pregnant and was scared. She was considering leaving him and would like help to do so.

Discussion

Initial interventions should include asking Claire if she would like to be registered as a "no-information" patient in the system so that her significant other cannot easily find her. Her physical injuries and psychological condition should be evaluated by a medical provider, and hospital staff should help coordinate outside resources and help with a safe discharge plan. This can include help from a forensic nurse, social worker, mental health specialist, and local advocacy agency.

Leaving an abusive relationship can be the most lethal time in the relationship. Pregnancy is also a risk factor for escalating violence in a relationship. It is essential to make sure that Claire has a sound and confidential discharge plan, adequate resources, and emergency contacts. Consider writing a few important resource phone numbers on a small piece of paper that Claire can conceal. She may not feel comfortable taking her discharge papers home if it contains information that could trigger her spouse, including information on domestic violence. Claire may be worried about custody issues since she is currently pregnant. Most domestic violence advocacy agencies have attorneys on staff to help with divorce, child custody, immigration, and more. The patient should be provided a contact to be sure this hurdle is not one she feels she cannot overcome.

There are various prediction tools that can be used by law enforcement or social workers to predict the likelihood that an offender will assault the victim again in the future. This can be a very eye-opening experience for the victim and help them see their situation and risk in a different light. These tools include The Ontario Domestic Assault Risk Assessment (ODARA), Spousal Assault Risk Assessment (SARA), Brief Spousal Assault Form for the Assessment of Risk (B-SAFER), Domestic Violence Screening Inventory (DVSI), and Danger Assessment (DA).[21-23] ODARA (or any other Risk Assessment Tool[24]) must be followed up with creating a safety plan by a trained social worker or advocate.

It is recommended that Claire file for a protection order or a no-contact order. Neither of these is usually an immediate order, so health care providers should advise the patient that they can contact law enforcement if they feel unsafe, even though they do not have a protection order in place yet. It is also important to recognize that being served a protection order can sometimes cause the perpetrator to escalate in temper and violence.

Case Study 3-2

Sara was a 44-year-old female who had been seen multiple times in the ED for the chief complaint of domestic assault. She always presented intoxicated and had a similar history of assault each time. She stated that her significant other would also get drunk and he would become physically aggressive. The argument usually started by accusing Sara of looking at or talking to another man and then would progress to a physical assault. During a previous ED visit, the patient had stated that she was pushed into a mirror which shattered. The patient did not present with visible injuries at the most recent visit.

Discussion

Sara and her significant other both abused alcohol, a known risk factor for interpersonal violence. Her partner has displayed jealousy and poor anger control, both risk factors for perpetrating interpersonal violence. Sara was allowed to sober in the ED so that hospital staff could complete a thorough assessment and create a safe discharge plan. Upon sobering, the patient stated she had nowhere else to go as she and her partner were both homeless. Shelters were contacted and a local shelter had availability for her. The hospital social worker or community advocate responded to the hospital to create a confidential and safe discharge plan and follow-up. Sara was provided with transportation to the shelter. She was provided with cab vouchers to the advocacy office for the next day so that they could meet with her and coordinate next steps once she had been able to sleep and could participate in a plan to help her find a safer and stable environment. They also helped her seek treatment for alcohol abuse. The more support systems in place for Sara, the better her chance of moving forward from this abusive situation.

Summary

There is considerable overlap in risk factors when assessing victims of interpersonal violence and their perpetrators. Exposure to and development of many of these risk factors begin in childhood homes. People who witness family violence in childhood are more likely to experience interpersonal violence as an adult. Children with higher ACE scores have more difficulty with healthy adult relationships. ACEs and poor parenting can lead to the development of maladaptive schemas, which increases a person's risk for experiencing interpersonal violence.

Prevention techniques should include implementation of programs that support parents to create a healthy home environment. Such programs may include classes on parenting, coping skills, and conflict resolution. In addition, strong community support can help support children who are experiencing neglect and violence at home. Communities can provide a safe place for survivors of interpersonal violence to recover and heal. Counseling can help people process trauma and learn more effective coping skills. Programs and therapy for alcohol and other substance abuse can make a difference in the cycle of violence.

Assessment should begin in the pediatrician's office and continue through the lifespan. Medical providers should feel comfortable assessing risk and talking about resources for interpersonal violence. Practitioners should encourage and facilitate change of modifiable risk factors. Substance abuse treatment is recommended and a variety of treatment options should be discussed with the patient to try to ensure participation and success. Recommending inpatient rehab to a victim/survivor who has children or who must work to provide for their family may not be realistic. However, they may be open to outpatient therapy or medications that can aid in cessation of use for alcohol or other substances. Being aware of unmodifiable risk factors can help practitioners recognize signs of interpersonal violence. The best way to support a victim/survivor is to build trust, educate them about their options, and give them choices for their therapy. Providers can generate hope by educating themselves and their communities about how to disrupt cycles of violence and how to support people when they are experiencing interpersonal violence.

References

1. Intimate partner violence. World Health Organization. 2022. https://apps.who.int/violence-info/intimate-partner-violence/
2. Udmuangpia T, Yu M, Laughon K, Saywat T, Bloom T. Prevalence, risks, and health consequences of intimate partner violence during pregnancy among young women: a systematic review. *Pac Rim Int J Nurs Res.* 2020;24(3):412-428.
3. Risk and protective factors. Centers for Disease Control and Prevention. Updated 2024. https://www.cdc.gov/intimate-partner-violence/risk-factors/?CDC_
4. Capaldi D, Knoble N, Shortt J, Kim H. A systematic review of risk factors for intimate partner violence. *Partner Abuse.* 2012;3(2):231-280. doi:10.1891/1946-6560.3.2.231
5. Statistics. National Coalition Against Domestic Violence. 2021. https://ncadv.org/statistics
6. Yakubovich AR, Stöckl H, Murray J, et al. Risk and protective factors for intimate partner violence against women: systematic review and meta-analyses of prospective-longitudinal studies. *Am J Public Health.* 2018;108(7):e1-e11. doi:10.2105/ajph.2018.304428
7. Chisholm C, Bullock L, Freguson J. Intimate partner violence and pregnancy: epidemiology and impact. *Am J Obstet Gynecol.* 2017;217(2):141-144. doi:10.1016/j.ajog.2017.05.042
8. Alhusen J, Ray E, Sharps P, Bullock L. Intimate partner violence during pregnancy: maternal and neonatal outcomes. *J Womens Health.* 2015;24(1):100-106. doi:10.1089%2Fjwh.2014.4872
9. LGBT domestic violence fact sheet. Center for American Progress. 2012. https://cdn.americanprogress.org/wp-content/uploads/2012/12/domestic_violence.pdf
10. Stiles-Shields C, Carroll RA. Same-sex domestic violence: prevalence, unique aspects, and clinical implications. *J Sex Marital Ther.* 2015;41(6):636-648. doi:10.1080/0092623X.2014.958792
11. Rollè L, Giardina G, Caldarera AM, Gerino E, Brustia P. When intimate partner violence meets same sex couples: a review of same sex intimate partner violence. *Front Psychol.* 2018;9:1506. doi:10.3389%2Ffpsyg.2018.01506
12. Vest JR, Catlin TK, Chen JJ, Brownson RC. Multistate analysis of factors associated with intimate partner violence. *Am J Prev Med.* 2002;22(3):156-164. doi:10.1016/s0749-3797(01)00431-7
13. Sanvictores T, Mendez M. *Types of Parenting Styles and Effects on Children.* StatPearls Publishing; 2023. https://www.ncbi.nlm.nih.gov/books/NBK568743/

14. The ACE study. Pinetree Institute. Accessed March 15, 2023. https://pinetreeinstitute.org/aces/

15. Protective factors and adverse childhood experiences. US Department of Health and Human Services. 2023. Accessed November 5, 2023. https://www.childwelfare.gov/topics/preventing/preventionmonth/about/protective-factors-aces/

16. Sanderson M, Mouton CP, Cook M, Liu J, Blot WJ, Hargreaves MK. Adverse childhood experiences and chronic disease risk in the southern community cohort study. *J Health Care Poor Underserved.* 2021;32(3):1384-1402. doi: 10.1353/hpu.2021.0139

17. Lockwood G. Schema therapy central concepts. International Society of Schema Therapy. 2008. https://schematherapysociety.org/Schema-Therapy

18. Taşkale N, Soygüt G. Risk factors for women's intimate partner violence victimization: an examination from the perspective of the schema therapy model. *J Fam Viol.* 2017;32:3-12. doi:10.1007/s10896-016-9855-6

19. Sójta K, Margulska A, Jóźwiak-Majchrzak W, Grażka A, Grzelczak K, Strzelecki D. Cognitive–affective risk factors of female intimate partner violence victimization: the role of early maladaptive schemas and strategic emotional intelligence. *Brain Sci.* 2023;13(7):1118. doi:10.3390/brainsci13071118

20. Protective factors for domestic violence survivors: a pathway to more opportunities. Children's Bureau Learning & Coordination Center. Accessed November 5, 2023. https://cblcc.acf.hhs.gov/

21. ODARA scoring form. Official Site of the State of New Jersey. 2010. Accessed November 5, 2023. https://www.nj.gov/lps/dcj/agguide/directives/ODARA-Scoring-Form.pdf

22. Jung S, Himmen MK. A field study on the police use of the Ontario Domestic Assault Risk Assessment (ODARA). *Journal of Threat Assessment and Management.* 2022;9(4):204-217. doi:10.1037/tam0000175

23. Hilton N, Pham A, Jung S, Nunes K, Ennis L. Risk scores and reliability of the SARA, SARA-V3, B-SAFER, and ODARA among intimate partner violence (IPV) cases referred for threat assessment. *Police Pract Res.* 2020;22(1):157-172. doi:10.1080/15614263.2020.1798235

24. Intimate partner violence risk assessment tools: a review. Government of Canada, Department of Justice. Updated December 8, 2021. www.justice.gc.ca/eng/rp-pr/cj-jp/fv-vf/rr12_8/a.html

Chapter 4

General Indicators of Interpersonal Violence in Women's Health

Margit B. Gerardi, PhD, APRN, WHNP, PMHNP-BC
Olivia Yeargain, MPH, MSN, APRN, PMHNP-BC
Tracy G. Senterfitt, MSN, APRN, PMHNP-BC

Objectives

After reviewing this chapter, the reader will be able to:

1. *Define domestic violence (DV).*
2. *Cite the most common indicators of DV.*
3. *Explain how community and societal factors influence DV prevalence using the sociopsychological perspective.*
4. *Describe why those experiencing DV might not be identified by health care and social service professionals.*

Introduction

Those who provide services in health care or social service settings commonly see individuals in their practices who have experienced or are currently experiencing DV. DV is manifested by 4 types of behaviors: physical violence, sexual violence, threats of physical or sexual violence, and psychological/emotional abuse. The Centers for Disease Control and Prevention (CDC) uses the following definitions for these behaviors, and, to standardize definitions, this chapter will use these CDC definitions as well[1]:

— ***Physical violence:*** The intentional use of physical force with the potential for causing death, disability, injury, or harm.

— ***Sexual violence:*** A deliberate or threatened action or behavior of sexual aggression directed toward a person with an intention to control, humiliate, or harm by another individual. Threats of physical or sexual violence use words, gestures, or weapons to communicate the intent to cause death, disability, injury, or physical harm.

— ***Psychological/emotional violence:*** Involves trauma to the survivor caused by acts, threats of acts, or coercive tactics.

— ***Stalking:*** Harassing or threatening behavior that an individual engages in repeatedly, such as following a person, appearing at a person's home or place of business, making harassing phone calls, leaving written messages or objects, or vandalizing a person's property.

Oftentimes, psychological or emotional violence is the beginning of a continuum of behaviors that commence with an escalation of relationship tensions progressing to emotional mistreatment, then further escalating to battering and eventually to violence. The absence of caring and respectful partner behaviors is just as powerful in creating an emotionally abusive experience as openly abusive behaviors.[2] Furthermore, emotional abuse is a dynamic event that encompasses multiple culminations, secondary physical and mental health symptoms, and quality of life issues that extend well beyond the immediate abuse experience.

DV crosses socioeconomic strata, ethnic groups, and opposite- as well as same-sex relationships. In every human culture, in every race, and in every nation, regardless of economic group, educational level, religious preference, or social strata, DV occurs. Both women and men can be survivors and perpetrators of DV. When women engage in DV, however, it often occurs as a reciprocal event in an argument or self-protection in the context of victimization. Kelly & Johnson[3] note that female DV usually manifests in situational couple violence rather than the coercive controlling violence often exhibited by male abusers. ***Situational couple violence*** occurs when 1 or both partners in a relationship handle conflict with violence in reaction to specific events and involve more minor acts of aggression. ***Coercive controlling violence*** occurs when a perpetrator attempts to reduce a person's autonomy and self-esteem through the use of intimidation and humiliation. Women who perpetrate violence as adolescents or young adults often have childhood experiences of violence.

Theoretical Framework

The ***socio-ecological model*** offers a means to see the "gestalt" when considering important individual aspects that influence violence in the lives of survivors and their families. Many organizations and individuals have adopted the socio-ecological model as the framework to both understand and target interventions toward preventing violence in the United States (**Figure 4-1**).[4] The framework consists of multiple interacting levels to understand the relationship between violence and potential prevention strategies.

Domestic Violence Socio-Ecological Model

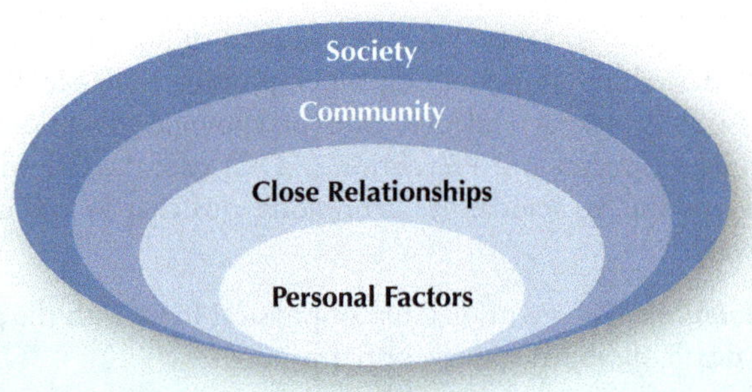

Figure 4-1

Figure 4-1. *Gerardi model of domestic violence (adapted from Bronfenbrenner's Ecological Systems Theory).*

The first level of the socio-ecological model is personal or individual risk factors for violence, which include an individual's unique psychological characteristics; physical factors including age, income level, education level, substance abuse or history of substance abuse; and the immediate physical setting, such as one's home. The next level examines close relationships that may also increase the risk for becoming either a perpetrator or a survivor of DV. These relationships may be close friends, partners, or family members. Prevention strategies for this level would be aimed at mentoring and the creation of peer prevention programs. Community is the third level of the socio-ecological model, and it seeks to identify the neighborhood, school, or workplace. This is where social relationships occur outside of the family unit and close friendships. This could involve a woman interacting with a health care provider at a clinic setting, education, or social support. Societal norms, strategies, and policies are affected at this level of impact. The fourth and last level of the socio-ecological model is society. Looking with a broader perspective, societal factors can create a climate that either repels or encourages DV. Other factors evaluated at this level include educational, health, economic, and societal policies.

Personal Risk Factors for Domestic Violence

Personal risk factors for DV include prior experiences of adverse childhood events, young age, senescence, pregnancy, chronic diseases or conditions, and disability (**Figure 4-2**). Screening for these at-risk groups should be individualized to each practice setting.

Personal Risk Factors Associated with Domestic Violence

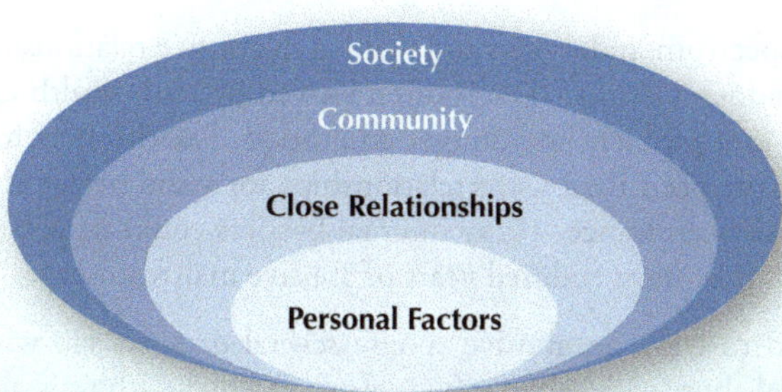

- Low self-esteem
- Young age
- Aggressive or delinquent behavior as a child
- Borderline personality traits
- Unemployment/ economic stress
- History of experiencing poor parenting or harsh physical discipline as a child
- Limited resources
- Heavy alcohol or drug use
- Prior history of being physically abusive
- Anger and hostility
- Emotional dependence and insecurity
- Victim of childhood abuse, neglect
- Low academic achievement
- Depression
- Antisocial personality traits
- Few friends, isolation
- Belief in strict gender roles
- Pregnancy

Figure 4-2

Figure 4-2. *Personal risk factors associated with DV.*

Adverse Childhood Experiences

Felitti and colleagues[5] were among the first researchers to establish a link between a child's exposure to adverse childhood experiences (ACEs) and later increased risk for health risk behaviors, disease, and death in adulthood. When protective factors are not sufficient to mitigate these childhood stressors, chronic neuroendocrine and immune system dysregulation and disruption in healthy brain development can arise. There is also now a growing body of research which posits that experiencing early ACEs (eg, physical, psychological, or sexual abuse, neglect, household/environment hardship and instability, family abuse) is also associated with a higher probability of experiencing subsequent DV as well as depression and post-traumatic stress disorder (PTSD) symptoms when in romantic relationships.[6]

Very Young Women

Just by being young and inexperienced, very young women (ages 10-17) are considered a vulnerable population and may experience abuse when entering new romantic relationships.

Adolescents may lack skills to create or negotiate healthy boundaries when meeting potential romantic partners. Even if they possess these social and relationship building skills, abusers may still target adolescents for opportunistic sexual gratification and dominance. Adolescents have limited skills to navigate complex relationships, especially those involving controlling and abusive partners at this developmental phase of their lives. For female adolescents, sexual behavior is most often linked to a desire for emotional commitment with another, while males typically view their early experimentation as more casual and directly fulfilling of sexual needs. The disparity between gender-based meanings of sexual behaviors may lead to greater sexual risk taking and vulnerability for females to enhance perceived relationship intimacy. Adolescents in sexual relationships with abusive partners are also at risk for unplanned pregnancy. Within age discordant relationships (ie, one partner being older), there can also be a disproportionate amount of control by the older member of the couple (typically the male), thereby perpetuating the cycle of violence and adverse sexual health outcomes.[7]

When women experience DV in their adolescent years, they are much less likely to disclose this to health care providers or other professionals who they encounter. Professionals in health care settings or service agencies need to create an environment that facilitates safe disclosure and discussion of adolescent sexual experiences. Disclosure may enhance the likelihood of a more positive outcome for adolescent DV survivors. The ability to disclose safely to another individual regarding DV and unwanted sexual contact may allow for a reframing of traumatic life events in a manner that fosters decreased shame and stigmatization. Another benefit of disclosure has been noted in sexual risk behavior reduction.

Aging

On the other end of the age spectrum, older men and women in abusive relationships are commonly considered "hidden victims." DV is often viewed by both health care professionals and the public as a problem of younger adulthood. Practitioners may encounter individuals who have been in abusive relationships for years before they disclose their experiences or seek assistance. Many internal barriers could be present with elder survivors of DV, as they have endured years of abusive maltreatment.

Women may have attempted to leave an abusive spouse several decades ago when conversations regarding spousal abuse were taboo, often secret, and met with resistance on several fronts. This may be the group of women that are least likely to report abuse to law enforcement officials or to those in legal settings. Likewise, older men who experience DV may not have sought help because of their lifetime experiences of stigma, shame, and gender role stereotypes.

Feelings of hopelessness, powerlessness, emotional gridlock, secrecy, and self-blame may reduce older people's ability to access help and disclose their experiences of violence.[8] They may have also stayed in abusive relationships for years, unable to leave for a variety of reasons ranging from economic ones to an internalized belief that staying was better for the sake of their children.

When caring for older individuals, it is important to give time, compassion, and a private setting to discuss their satisfaction with their present relationship. When an individual may have chosen to stay with an abuser, health care and social service professionals often have dismissive attitudes and fail to discuss options to help them stay safely within the relationship. Although getting a person out of a dangerous relationship is often a first response, older persons may not feel comfortable leaving a partner of several decades. Rather than close the window of opportunity to help older individuals, assisting them with disclosure and counseling services may help them break the cycle of violence.

Disabilities and Domestic Violence

People experiencing physical or intellectual disabilities (ID) make up diverse groups that are at heightened risk for DV. Disabilities increase the risk for all types of DV in a dose-dependent manner and this association has been repeatedly reported. In some cases, physical disabilities and IDs are the direct result of trauma from DV. Those who are physically disabled are less likely to seek help or disclose abuse in health care settings for a variety of reasons ranging from fear of abuser retribution to heightened vulnerability due to isolation. Many centers that do provide services for people with disabilities may overlook screening for DV and resources, or facilities for care, if such occurs.[9]

Taggert and colleagues[10] reported that women with an ID were at a much higher risk of DV than those without an ID. It was also noted that women with an ID were also 1.5 times more likely to have experienced any form of violence in their childhood. As is typical, they then experience violence with an abusive partner and the cycle of violence continues. This is concerning for health and social service providers, as those experiencing ID are frequently not gender-focused, and like those experiencing DV who are physically disabled, opportunities to identify and intervene with DV are often missed.

Close Relationships

Intimacy in relationships can be defined by physical or emotional closeness, or both, and can exist in many forms. Despite the term "domestic" used in DV, intimate relationships are not necessarily bound by cohabitation, marital, or relationship status. Furthermore, it is important to note that DV does exist in open, polygamist, and polyamorous relationships. When there is a relationship between 2 or more people that is intimate, there is the possibility of a loving, respectful, trusting relationship on the one hand. On the other, there is the possibility of DV as one partner tries to control the other(s). Common relational risk factors are listed in **Figure 4-3**. In cases of DV, factors that once created or defined the relationship are no longer based on mutual trust and respect.

Figure 4-3. *Close relationship risk factors for DV.*

Close Relationship Risk Factors for Domestic Violence

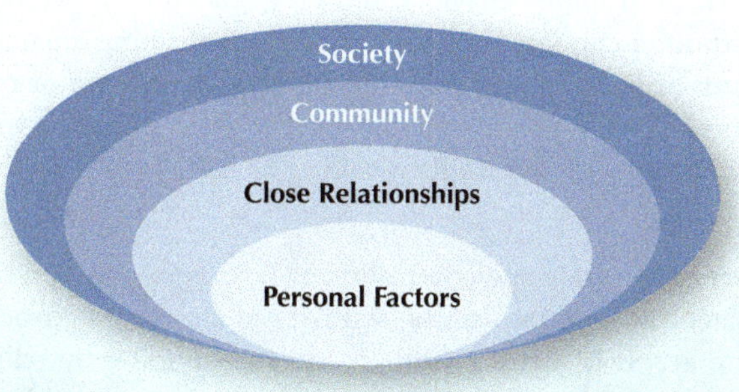

- Marital conflict - tension, struggles
- Marital instability- divorce, separations
- Dominance and control over relationship by one partner
- Economic stress
- Substance abuse by partner
- Unhealthy family interactions and relationships

Figure 4-3

Marital or Relationship Instability and Breakdown

DV is often sparked by 1 member of the relationship who wishes to force the other member of the relationship to take actions that are not of their own choosing and are often harmful physically or emotionally. Early in the relationship, this may result in marital conflict and tension, but quickly escalates to unhealthy family relationships and interactions. Perpetrators may take power and control in the relationship by "using coercion and threats, intimidation, emotional abuse, isolation, minimizing, denying, blaming, and male privilege."[11] The perpetrator may also directly threaten children, threaten flight with them, or use them to spread misinformation.

Further degradation of the familial relationship results in marital instability and ultimately separation and divorce, adding economic stress to already strained marital and family relationships. It is during these times of stress that emotional and physical violence may surface for the first time. The slow and insidious nature of this development anchors the abused partner in the degrading relationship as they believe it will not happen again or that they "deserved" the violence because of their behavior.

Professionals providing services are often at a loss to understand why an individual would remain in a violent relationship. Often, they stop offering counseling and related services when a person does not immediately leave an abusive partner, thinking that they are unwilling to act. As care providers understand the reasons that survivors choose to leave or stay in an abusive relationship, the complex nature of that decision may make continued caring and intervention attempts more frequent.

Effect of Domestic Violence on Men

Men are affected by DV in both heterosexual and homosexual relationships, as previously described, although it is underreported in part due to stigma, both internalized and externalized, as well as barriers to reporting and obtaining care. Gay and bisexual men are especially vulnerable, given their increased risk for DV, coupled with the lack of appropriate DV screening tools for men.[12] They may also feel pressured to avoid further stigmatization of the LGBTQIA+ community or reinforce internalized stereotypes of weakness in gay men.[13] Thus, it is important to address limitations to help-seeking behaviors and support and encourage all male victims of DV to seek help. As Huntley et al[14] identified, there are 9 themes affecting help-seeking behavior among males experiencing DV: fear of disclosure, challenge to masculinity, commitment to relationship, diminished confidence/despondency, invisibility/perception of services, initial contact, confidentiality, appropriate professional approaches, and inappropriate professional approaches. Additionally, the assumption that DV is mainly physical can dissuade male victims to disclose their encounters of abuse.

For men in homosexual relationships, a 2013 study by Stephenson et al[12] identified 3 additional domains of DV not found in screening tools, but which reflect the shared experiences of gay and bisexual men who reported DV. Identified domains include monitoring behaviors, controlling behaviors, and HIV-related DV, including being forced to have sex without a condom and suspecting or confirming a partner is lying about their HIV status or intentionally transmitting HIV. A perpetrator may also threaten to disclose a victim's HIV-positive status, prevent them from accessing medication or care, or assume economic control by taking advantage of a victim's poor health status.[15]

DV from female perpetrators can include coercive threats or reports to police, Child Protective Services or legal action, communication with the male victim through their/his children, restricting access to shared children, emotional abuse by telling him he is not the father of their children or belittling childcare efforts, in addition to physical abuse, sexual abuse, and monitoring or isolative behaviors. There is also the "weaponisation of masculinity," in which gendered norms are used to demean or coerce. From female perpetrators, this might include forcing the man into "specific responsibilities based on strict traditional gender roles without any negotiation and under fear of consequences"[15] or belittling his masculinity if he does not do certain things or do them in a certain way.

Physical indicators of DV with male victims were identified in a recent retrospective study by Wörmann and colleagues.[16] Male victims were more likely to have injuries, primarily blunt force but also sharp, on the upper body half, primarily arms, then face and neck (for blunt trauma), chest (for sharp force), back, and skull. Injuries from female perpetrators were more likely scratch and bite marks, as well as from instrumental violence, including boiling water, knives, and household items. Injuries from male perpetrators more often involved manual strangulation. Instrumental violence was more common in ongoing relationships compared to separated couples. Finally, men who experienced blunt force trauma were less likely to report abuse to police or seek medical care.

Community/Societal Factors

Patients in today's care settings come from diverse cultural backgrounds and geographically distinct homelands. Survivors and their families may have a different worldview and set of experiences regarding intimate relationships. How women are valued in society also varies widely. In regions of the world where communities and nations have been ravaged by warfare, this is especially problematic. Women are often traumatized by societal violence, experiencing rape by invading aggressors and then devalued by their partners and the community upon their perpetrator's departure. Additionally, using resource control or desire for acquisition as a causal theory of violence risk can be demonstrated through violence noted in nations that are experiencing economic inequity or increasing population density.[17]

Barzelatto[18] asserts that violence stems from unbalanced power, injustice, and lack of democracy in society as a whole. Members of groups, cultures, and societies that have positive attitudes toward male dominance of females will be more likely to tolerate or accept DV. At a microsystem level, gender-based violence against women is thought to share macrosystem causes as well. Special groups of concern for violence risk would include female adolescents and sex workers who are deemed more vulnerable due to both their limited resources and power base. **Figure 4-4** depicts the community or societal factors beyond the individual or the individual relationships that can encourage or discourage DV.

Community and Societal Risk Factors for Domestic Violence

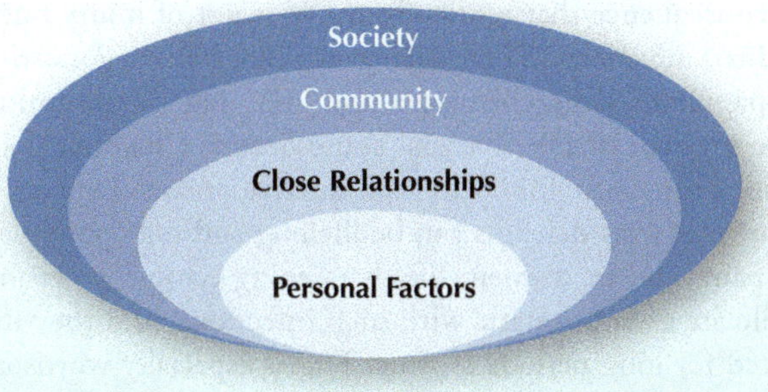

Poverty and associated factors:
Overcrowding

Low social capital:
Lack of institutions, relationships, or community social interactions

Weak community sanctions against DV:
Unwilling to intervene in situations where they witness violence

Traditional norms:
Women stay at home and do not work, men support the family and make decisions

Figure 4-4

Figure 4-4. *Community and societal risk factors for DV.*

A community-level analysis of violence risk also involves examining the nature of person-to-person violence from a sociopsychological perspective. Although school violence gets noticeable press and media attention, children and adolescents are more likely to exhibit, witness, or be victimized in their home or community. Bandura[19] and others have suggested that violence is learned and repeated by observation and by the modeling of displayed aggressive behavior and acts of violence. As an unfortunate aftermath, Foshee and colleagues[20] suggest that children who watch their parents use violence to resolve problems or conflict will be more likely to engage in or see violence as acceptable in later adolescent or adult relationships.

Risk for violence has also been related to environmental factors. Childhood exposure to a dysfunctional family unit may also be associated in other ways with the development of later violent tendencies in adolescence and adulthood. Tarter and colleagues[21] identified that future risk for violence is associated with childhood exposure to parents who abuse substances, have psychiatric disorders, or who provide inadequate supervision. Family instability, maternal rejection, marital conflict, and an absent or rejecting father have also been associated with a greater potential for male child members to later engage in violence or for female child members to experience DV in future relationships.

Consequences of Domestic Violence

Physical Indicators

The physical consequences of DV are most often thought of as injury, specifically trauma, to the survivor. The most common consequences are listed in **Table 4-1**. As the number of times a person is on the receiving end of DV increases, the encounters are then associated with increasingly severe injury. In the beginning, physical violence may be a shove or slap, which then progresses to a single hit, punch, or kick, and then further progresses into multiple hits, punches, or kicks. Eventually, there may be a result of the worst possible outcome: death at the hands of the perpetrator.

It is important to recognize patterns of acute trauma related to DV in order to identify and intervene when DV is covert. In health care settings, assessments should be given to any woman with trauma to the upper extremities, head, neck, and face, as these regions are the most common injury sites for DV. Most traumas to women will be inflicted by the abuser's use of slapping with their hand or striking with their fist and involve soft tissue injury, using the face or head as a target for attack. Zygomatic complex, orbital blow-out, mandibular, nasal, and malar fractures, and intracranial injuries are the most prevalent facial injuries and account for the majority of severe trauma associated with DV.[22] Strangulation is experienced by over 1/2 of DV survivors, yet often remains a covert marker of DV in clinical settings.[23] Upper extremity injuries are common sites for dislocations, fractures, and soft tissue injury that is seen when survivors attempt to use defensive posturing during an attack.[24]

A second type of physical consequence that results from DV is not of injury but of disease. All sexually transmitted infections (STIs), such as syphilis, herpes, gonorrhea, bacterial vaginosis, human papilloma virus, chlamydia, and HIV may be transmitted from the perpetrator to the survivor of DV if sexual abuse occurs. Chlamydial and gonococcal cervical infections can cause injury to reproductive organs. Damage to a female's fallopian tubes or male's vas deferens can be lifelong and may potentially lead to infertility, chronic pain, and in women, life-threatening ectopic pregnancy. Unfortunately, many people are asymptomatic with such infections, and they may go undetected and untreated for long periods of time. This is especially worrisome because partners who are abusive may not reveal their sexual contact with other individuals, thereby placing their unknowing partners at marked risk. This lag between time of infection and time of treatment leads to greater rates of disease transmission and increased health risks.

Furthermore, while there are direct effects of physical violence and sexual assault on survivors, there are also indirect effects. Some of these indirect effects are short-lived while others are long-lasting. These often hidden consequences include suicidal thoughts, suicide attempts, depression, anxiety, pregnancy, and resultant adverse effects on maternal and neonatal outcomes.[25] The chronic stress that the survivor experiences as a result of DV affects the endocrine and immune systems, and these resulting consequences might be: fibromyalgia, gynecological disorders, irritable bowel syndrome, central nervous system disorders, STIs, gastrointestinal disorders, and heart and circulatory disorders.

Morbidity related to pregnant women who are abused must take into account 2 victims, the mother and the baby. Often, the gravid abdomen is kicked, punched, or hit, which may result in spontaneous loss of the pregnancy, abruption, late entry into prenatal care, stillbirth, premature labor, delivery, and, of course, femicide.[26,27]

Psychological Consequences

The experience of DV commonly results in psychological consequences to its survivors.[25] It is often difficult to identify whether psychological dysfunction or stressors were present prior to abuse or whether the experience of violence was the etiologic factor in the development of mental health problems. It has been well established that when comparing those experiencing DV to those who have not experienced violence, a significant difference in their experience of negative psychological sequelae was supported.[28] Common psychological consequences are depression, suicidal behavior, anxiety disorders including PTSD, and substance abuse. When abuse occurs in an intimate relationship, emotional and affective changes of personality and psychological

Table 4-1. Health Consequences of Domestic Violence[12,16,25,29]

Physical	Psychological and Behavioral
— Abdominal/thoracic injuries	— Alcohol and drug abuse
— Bite marks/scratches	— Belittling masculinity
— Bruises and welts	— Depression and anxiety
— Chronic pain syndromes	— Eating and sleep disorders
— Disability	— Feelings of shame and guilt
— Fibromyalgia	— Phobias and panic disorder
— Fractures	— Physical inactivity
— Gastrointestinal disorders	— Poor self-esteem
— Instrumental violence	— PTSD
— Irritable bowel syndrome	— Psychosomatic disorders
— Lacerations and abrasions	— Smoking
— Ocular damage	— Suicidal behavior and self-harm
— Reduced physical functioning	— Unsafe sexual behavior
— Sexual and reproductive	— Fatal health consequences
— Gynecological disorders	— AIDS-related mortality
— Infertility	— Maternal mortality
— Pelvic inflammatory disease	— Homicide/femicide
— Pregnancy complications/miscarriage	— Suicide
— Sexual dysfunction	
— STIs including HIV/AIDS	
— Strangulation	
— Unsafe abortion	

Adapted from: Heise L, Garcia-Moreno C. Violence by intimate partners. In: Krug E, Dahlberg LL, Mercy Ja, Zwi AB, Lozano R, eds. World Report on Violence and Health. Geneva, Switzerland: World Health Organization; 2002: 87-121.[29]

milieu can arise from this victimization. These changes can include lowered self-esteem, inability to trust romantic partners or others, fear of intimacy, anger, shame, helplessness, emotional detachment, and the intrusive and recurrent remembrances of degrading experiences in the survivor's mind.[11,25] Further consequences are listed in **Table 4-1**.

Long-term Health Consequences

Relationships marked by months to years of DV can lead to activation of the hypothalamic-pituitary-adrenal (HPA) axis and dysregulation of normal cortisol production, which has been linked to cardiovascular disease and other disease states such as diabetes.[30] Further, stressors experienced in DV can also initiate immune dysregulation across a wide range of immune responses, especially when this stress is chronic. When women experience DV, the number of unhealthy behaviors and long-term, serious health consequences are significantly greater. Increased cardiovascular risk (eg, cholesterol, stroke, heart disease) was demonstrated in higher adjusted odds ratios for women experiencing DV versus risk for women who did not. Similarly, rates of joint disease and asthma were also higher in women who were abused.[30] The more severe the violence, the stronger the correlation to negative health behaviors by the survivors.

Case Studies

Case Study 4-1

A 31-year-old female veteran, Sarah, was recently discharged from the Army after 8 years of service. Her husband remained enlisted in the Army and recently returned from deployment after 6 months. During her intake, she scored a 14 on the Extended - Hurt, Insult, Threaten, Scream (E-HITS) screening tool in which a score greater than 10 is considered positive for experiencing DV. The provider broached the topic of DV with Sarah and she denied it, stating that her husband has never been physically aggressive with her. However, she cited several examples of persistent emotional and psychological abuse such as putting her down and humiliating her in front of her family, acting jealous, constantly accusing her of cheating, and calling her insulting names like "stupid" and "worthless." She also disclosed that she was a survivor of military sexual trauma by her commanding officer while enlisted, but never reported it for fear of losing her rank and other repercussions.

Discussion

Active military members and veterans have unique risk factors for DV and a higher prevalence rate of DV compared to civilians. Military values of discipline, obedience, authority, and a collective-over-personal priority contribute to this. Military members may also reside overseas or in isolated areas away from family and social support, thereby increasing the risk for DV. Additionally, survivors or their partners may have fixed-year contracts, receive housing or food from the military, and social support from friends who are also colleagues, making disclosure harder.[31,32]

A military setting may also make it harder for survivors of DV to seek care. This is because the military is self-contained; they have their own health care and judicial system. Members may avoid seeking help for mental health stressors and trauma, including DV, whilst on active duty, turning instead to maladaptive coping mechanisms like isolation or substance use.[31,32]

Case Study 4-2

A 27-year-old male, Aiden, worked as a marketing assistant at a large firm. Aiden is a cisgender man who identifies as gay. He presented for a routine visit and requested STI/HIV testing. Aiden revealed that he recently lost his job and was having difficulty obtaining a new one. In the interim, he was living with and relying on his partner of 1.5 years for financial support. Aiden's score on the E-HITS screening tool was negative, meaning it was a score less than 10. However, the provider knew that the current screening tools to identify DV in males were not wholly effective. Thus, the provider decided to question Aiden further about his relationship.

As the provider performed Aiden's physical examination, he noted bruising to his upper left arm and tenderness to his lower back. When questioned about the injuries, Aiden revealed that his partner threw a cell phone at him during an argument last week. He also revealed that he lost his job in part due to the actions of his partner, who showed up at Aiden's workplace several times to check on his whereabouts, pressured him to quit his job, and recently hid his car keys so he could not leave for work. Aiden reported further frequent arguments with his partner, during which small items were thrown at him (eg, TV remote, water glass, spatula). His partner also had recently begun to refuse to wear a condom during sex, and he threatened to reveal Aiden's sexual orientation to members of his family.

Discussion

In an effort to avoid further stigmatization of the LGBTQIA+ community, reinforcing stereotypes of homosexual men, or because of sexual minority stress, Aiden may have had difficulty reporting his experience with DV. Furthermore, men in general are less likely to report abuse as they tend to be less informed about DV due to a lack of support services that target or include them.[16] Other help-seeking barriers for men may be the fear of disclosure, challenges to masculinity, their commitment to the relationship, diminished confidence/despondency, initial contact issues, confidentiality fears, and inappropriate professional approaches.[14]

Bruising to Aiden's upper arm and the tenderness of his back, the financial stressors of losing his job, and his request for STI/HIV testing are all psychosocial/physical indicators that should raise a health care provider's suspicion for DV. Additionally, Aiden disclosing that his partner refused to wear a condom during sex was significant. This is because HIV infection is highly associated with DV among the population of men who have sex with men. HIV-related DV is an area of abuse that is often not included within screening tools. HIV-related DV includes lying about HIV status to a partner, not revealing HIV-positive status before sex, intentionally transmitting HIV, refusing to wear a condom during sex, threatening to reveal or actually revealing a person's HIV-positive status, and taking advantage of a partner's poor health status for financial or other gain.

Summary

Those in the social services and health care fields can make a difference through early assessment and intervention with patients and families of all kinds (ie, traditional, blended, nontraditional) who are affected by DV. Providers must be vigilant and ready to pick up on both subtle and overt indicators of DV victimization and take advantage of the available identification and assessment instruments in order to help target those who need it. It is also the survivor's decision on when to take action against their DV perpetrator. It has been well established that the most dangerous time for life-threatening injury and femicide/homicide related to DV is upon attempts to leave or when one has just recently left an abusive relationship. Furthermore, survivors may not be able to leave their relationship immediately, so it is important to establish a safety plan before they leave the practice setting. This safety plan will enable them to plan for contingencies and escape in a way that reduces harm to themselves, their children, other family members living with them, and their pets. In many larger cities, agencies dedicated to assisting victims of DV are available. In smaller cities and rural areas, it will be important to gather several referral sites and contact information from social service agencies and local shelters, and seek legal aid in advance of any anticipated need. Hotline numbers for telephone crisis intervention and information may also be useful. Lastly, as a survivor's rights and legal protection vary widely from state to state, it is imperative to know what each city and state will do to protect them.

References

1. Intimate partner violence. Centers for Disease Control and Prevention. 2021. Accessed December 22, 2021. https://www.cdc.gov/violenceprevention/intimatepartnerviolence/index.html

2. Bottoms BL, Peter-Hagene LC, Epstein MA, Wiley TR, Reynolds CE, Rudnicki AG. Abuse characteristics and individual differences related to disclosing childhood sexual, physical, and emotional abuse and witnessed domestic violence. *J Interpers Violence.* 2016;31(7):1308-1339. doi:10.1177/0886260514564155

3. Kelly J, Johnson M. Differentiation among types of intimate partner violence: research update and implications for interventions. *Fam Court Rev.* 2008;46: 476-499. doi:10.1111/j.1744-1617.2008.00215.x

4. Bronfenbrenner U. Interacting systems in human development. Research paradigms: present and future. In: Bronfenbrenner U, ed. *Making Human Beings Human: Bioecological Perspectives on Human Processes.* Cambridge University Press; 2005: 67-93.

5. Felitti VJ, Anda RF, Nordenberg D, et al. Relationship of childhood abuse and household dysfunction to many of the leading causes of death in adults. The Adverse Childhood Experiences (ACE) Study. *Am J Prev Med.* 1998;14(4):245-258. doi:10.1016/s0749-3797(98)00017-8

6. Willie TC, Kershaw T, Sullivan TP. The impact of adverse childhood events on the sexual and mental health of women experiencing intimate partner violence. *J Interpers Violence.* 2021;36(11-12):5145-5166. doi:10.1177/0886260518802852

7. Volpe EM, Hardie TL, Cerulli C, Sommers MS, Morrison-Beedy D. What's age got to do with it? Partner age difference, power, intimate partner violence, and sexual risk in urban adolescents. *J Interpers Violence*. 2013;28(10):2068-2087. doi:10.1177/0886260512471082

8. Weeks LE, Stilwell C, Gagnon D, Dupuis-Blanchard S, MacQuarrie C, Jackson LA. Initiatives to support older women who experience intimate partner violence. *Violence Against Women*. 2021;27(15-16):3011-3029. doi:10.1177/10778012 20988355

9. Ballan MS, Freyer MB, Powledge L. Intimate partner violence among men with disabilities: the role of health care providers. *Am J Mens Health*. 2017; 11(5):1436-1443. doi:10.1177/1557988315606966

10. Taggart L, McMillan R, Lawson A. Staffs' knowledge and perceptions of working with women with intellectual disabilities and mental health problems. *J Intellect Disabil Res*. 2010;54(1):90-100. doi:10.1111/j.1365-2788.2009.01211.x

11. Understanding the power and control wheel. Domestic Abuse Intervention Programs. Accessed December 22, 2021. https://www.theduluthmodel.org/wheels/

12. Stephenson R, Hall CD, Williams W, Sato K, Finneran C. Towards the development of an intimate partner violence screening tool for gay and bisexual men. *West J Emerg Med*. 2013;14(4):390-400. doi:10.5811/westjem.3.2013.15597

13. Rollè L, Giardina G, Caldarera AM, Gerino E, Brustia P. When intimate partner violence meets same sex couples: a review of same sex intimate partner violence. *Front Psychol*. 2018;9:1506. doi:10.3389/fpsyg.2018.01506

14. Huntley AL, Potter L, Williamson E, Malpass A, Szilassy E, Feder G. Help-seeking by male victims of domestic violence and abuse (DVA): a systematic review and qualitative evidence synthesis. *BMJ Open*. 2019;9(6):e021960. doi:10.1136/bmjopen-2018-021960

15. Martin L, Panteloudakis I. Toolkit for work with male victims of domestic abuse. Respect. 2019. https://setdab.org/wp-content/uploads/2019/06/Respect-Toolkit-for-Work-with-Male-Victims-of-Domestic-Abuse-2019.pdf

16. Wörmann X, Wilmes S, Seifert D, Anders S. Males as victims of intimate partner violence - results from a clinical-forensic medical examination centre. *Int J Legal Med*. 2021;135(5):2107-2115. doi:10.1007/s00414-021-02615-x

17. Krahé B. Violence against women. *Curr Opin Psychol*. 2018;19:6-10. doi:10.1016/j.copsyc.2017.03.017

18. Barzelatto J. Understanding sexual and reproductive violence: an overview. *Int J Gynaecol Obstet*. 1998;63:S13-S18. doi:10.1016/S0020-7292(98)00179-9

19. Bandura A, Ross D, Ross SA. Imitation of film-mediated aggressive models. *J Abnorm Soc Psychol*. 1963;66:3-11. doi:10.1037/h0048687

20. Foshee VA, McNaughton Reyes HL, Chen MS, et al. Shared risk factors for the perpetration of physical dating violence, bullying, and sexual harassment among adolescents exposed to domestic violence. *J Youth Adolesc*. 2016;45(4):672-686. doi:10.1007/s10964-015-0404-z

21. Tarter RE, Kirisci L, Vanyukov M, et al. Predicting adolescent violence: impact of family history, substance abuse, psychiatric history, and social adjustment. *Am J Psychiatry*. 2002;159(9):1541-1547. doi:10.1176/appi.ajp.159.9.1541

22. Porter A, Montgomery CO, Montgomery BE, Eastin C, Boyette J, Snead G. Intimate partner violence-related fractures in the United States: an 8 year review. *J Fam Violence*. 2019;34(7):601-609. doi:10.1007/s10896-018-0007-z

23. Messing JT, Patch M, Wilson JS, Kelen GD, Campbell J. Differentiating among attempted, completed, and multiple nonfatal strangulation in women experiencing intimate partner violence. *Womens Health Issues*. 2018;28(1):104-111. doi:10.1016/j.whi.2017.10.002

24. Thomas R, Dyer GSM, Tornetta Iii P, et al. Upper extremity injuries in the victims of intimate partner violence. *Eur Radiol.* 2021;31(8):5713-5720. doi:10.1007/s00330-020-07672-1

25. Karakurt G, Patel V, Whiting K, Koyutürk M. Mining electronic health records data: domestic violence and adverse health effects. *J Fam Violence*. 2017;32(1):79-87. doi:10.1007/s10896-016-9872-5

26. Finnbogadóttir H, Baird K, Thies-Lagergren L. Birth outcomes in a Swedish population of women reporting a history of violence including domestic violence during pregnancy: a longitudinal cohort study. *BMC Pregnancy Childbirth.* 2020;20(1):183. doi:10.1186/s12884-020-02864-5

27. Donovan BM, Spracklen CN, Schweizer ML, Ryckman KK, Saftlas AF. Intimate partner violence during pregnancy and the risk for adverse infant outcomes: a systematic review and meta-analysis. *BJOG*. 2016;123(8):1289-1299. doi:10.1111/1471-0528.13928

28. Hameed M, O'Doherty L, Gilchrist G, et al. Psychological therapies for women who experience intimate partner violence. *Cochrane Database Syst Rev*. 2020;7(7): CD013017. doi:10.1002/14651858.CD013017.pub2

29. Heise L, Garcia-Moreno C. Violence by intimate partners. In: Krug E, Dahlberg LL, Mercy JA, Zwi AB, Lozano R, eds. *World Report on Violence and Health.* World Health Organization; 2002:87-121.

30. Yim IS, Kofman YB. The psychobiology of stress and intimate partner violence. *Psychoneuroendocrinology*. 2019;105:9-24. doi:10.1016/j.psyneuen.2018.08.017

31. Kwan J, Sparrow K, Facer-Irwin E, Thandi G, Fear NT, MacManus D. Prevalence of intimate partner violence perpetration among military populations: a systematic review and meta-analysis. *Aggress Violent Behav*. 2020;53:101419. doi:10.1016/j.avb.2020.101419

32. Dichter ME, Wagner C, True G. Women veterans' experiences of intimate partner violence and non-partner sexual assault in the context of military service: implications for supporting women's health and well-being. *J Interpers Violence.* 2018;33(6):843-864. doi:10.1177/0886260516669166

The views expressed here are those of the authors and do not necessarily reflect the official policy or position of the US Department of Veterans Affairs.

Chapter 5

LGBTQIA+ Considerations

Jaclyn Rodriguez, BSN, BS, RN, SANE-A, SANE-P

Objectives

After reviewing this chapter, the reader will be able to:

1. *Identify key terms associated with the lesbian, gay, bisexual, transgender, queer/questioning, intersex, asexual/aromantic/agender (LGBTQIA+) community.*
2. *Identify the prevalence of interpersonal violence in the LGBTQIA+ community.*
3. *Understand the challenges that LGBTQIA+ victims may experience when disclosing abuse or seeking help.*
4. *Examine the unique forms of violence associated with LGBTQIA+ interpersonal violence.*

Introduction

The definitions of interpersonal and intimate partner violence (IPV) do not include any mention of an individual's gender or identity. LGBTQIA+ interpersonal violence can involve violence between same-gender or queer intimate partners as well as individuals who identify outside the gender binary of male and female. IPV has historically been strongly associated with heterosexual relationships and gendered roles (ie, male perpetrator and female victim). However, when a victim is part of the LGBTQIA+ community, the marginalized and often complicated aspects of their relationship are not reflected or understood within mainstream victim services.[1] Homophobia, heterosexism, transphobia, and biphobia create a context that impacts victims' experiences with their abusive partners, access to resources, and responses from support systems. These stigmas also affect what people have access to or can use to wield abusive power and control over their partners.[2] For example, many shelters only have beds for women, and they may not recognize a transgender woman as such because she was assigned male at birth, making it difficult for her to access necessary shelter services. Other problems that may arise include when the abusive partner can fool victim service agencies into believing that the victim was the one perpetrating the abuse, leading the victim to be barred from receiving important services.

Key Terms and Definitions

While the LGBTQIA+ acronym is a way to describe some of the common terms that may be used to identify the characteristics and attributes of communities and people, sometimes these terms can have multiple meanings. A key aspect of working with this community is to allow individuals to identify themselves and their community by utilizing terms that they feel most comfortable with. Providers should utilize active listening and respect to avoid offending, misunderstanding, misidentifying, or missing important information that is being shared. **Table 5-1** provides some of the terms that are helpful to know when working with a survivor who identifies as LGBTQIA+.

Table 5-1. LGBTQIA+[1-4]

Term	Definition
+	A plethora of other orientations and identities
AFAB	Assigned female at birth
AGAB	Assigned gender at birth
Agender (or Genderless)	A person who does not have a gender identity or whose gender identity is neutral
Ally	A person who advocates for or supports a marginalized or politicized group but is not a member of the group
AMAB	Assigned male at birth
Aromantic	An individual who experiences little or no romantic attraction
Asexual	An individual who, within the spectrum of sexuality, may not experience sexual attraction
Bigender	A person who has 2 gender identities or some combination of both
Biphobia	The systemic oppression of bisexual people specifically because they are not gay or heterosexual (eg, many bisexual people feel that they are forced to "choose" between 2 identities that do not fit them)
Bisexual	A sexual orientation that describes a person who is emotionally, romantically, and sexually attracted to people of their own gender and people of other genders
Bottom Surgery	The surgical alteration of a transgender person's genitals to align with their gender identity
Cisgender	A person whose gender identity corresponds to the gender assigned at birth (ie, a person who is not transgender)
Front Butt	An alternate term for an individual's genitals
Front Hole	A word that can be used to talk about internal genitals, sometimes referred to as a vagina
Gay	A term used in some cultural settings to represent males who are attracted to males in a romantic, erotic, and/or emotional sense. Not all men who engage in "same-sex behavior" identify as gay, and as such this label should be used with caution. This term is also used to refer to the LGBTQIA+ community as a whole or as an individual identity label for anyone who does not identify as heterosexual.
Gender Expression	The way a person externally performs or signifies their gender identity, especially through habits of dressing, grooming, behaving, or speaking
Gender-fluid	Noting or relating to a person whose gender identity or gender expression is not fixed and shifts over time or changes depending on the situation
Gender Identity	A person's internal sense of self and how they exist in the world, from the perspective of gender. This is a person's sense of being masculine, feminine, both, or neither gender. Only the person can identify this for themselves—it cannot be assigned by someone else.
Gender Nonconforming	A person whose gender identity differs from that which was assigned at birth, but may be more complex, fluid, multifaceted, or otherwise less clearly defined than a transgender person

(continued)

Table 5-1. LGBTQIA+[1-4] *(continued)*

Term	Definition
Gender queer (or Genderqueer)	A person whose gender identity is something other than male or female or whose gender presentation does not conform to socially defined male or female gender norms
Heteronormative	Behavior or attitudes consistent with traditional male or female gender roles and the assumption of heterosexuality as the norm
Heterosexism	The belief that heterosexual (ie, straight) relationships and people are the ideal and that they are better or more "normal" than queer relationships and people. Heterosexism also includes the denial that queer people even exist and the assumption that everyone is straight unless they indicate otherwise.
Homophobia	The systemic oppression of gay men, lesbians, and bisexual people because of their sexuality. Many people define homophobia to include all queer people.
Intersex	The term used for the 2% of individuals who are born with naturally occurring variations in chromosomes, hormones, genitalia, and other sex characteristics
Lesbian	A term used to describe female-identified people attracted romantically, erotically, and/or emotionally to other female-identified people
Nonbinary	A transgender or gender nonconforming person who identifies outside of the male/female gender binary; may include identities that are both male/female or neither male/female
Pangender	A person whose gender identity is not limited to 1 gender and who may feel like a member of all genders at the same time
Pansexual	Individuals whose attractions, whether emotional or sexual, are not limited by biological sex or gender
Queer	This term is often seen as blurring the boundaries between categories of sexual orientation and gender identity and can include gay, lesbian, bisexual, and transgender identities. A reclaimed word that historically has been a derogatory term, but which some LGBTQIA+ people now use from a place of power and self-identity.
Questioning	A person who is uncertain about or questioning their sexuality or gender identity
Sexual Orientation	Describes sexual attraction only and is not directly related to gender identity. The sexual orientation of transgender people should be defined by the individual. It is often described based on the lived gender; a transgender woman attracted to other women may identify as a lesbian, and a transgender man attracted to other men may identify as a gay man.
Top Surgery	The surgical alteration of a transgender person's chest, usually through double mastectomy or breast augmentation, to align with their gender identity
Transgender	A person whose gender identity differs from the sex that was assigned at birth. It may be abbreviated to "trans" and used as an umbrella term to describe a wide variety of gender identities including nonbinary, gender expansive, gender nonconforming, or transgender man/transgender woman. A transgender man is a person assigned female at birth who identifies as male; a transgender woman is assigned male at birth but identifies as female. A non-transgender person may be referred to as cisgender.
Transitioning	To move toward openly expressing one's gender identity, often by making changes to one's way of dressing, acting, or speaking, to one's pronouns, name, or legal gender marker, or to one's physical characteristics via hormone therapy and surgery

(continued)

Table 5-1. LGBTQIA+[1-4] *(continued)*

TERM	DEFINITION
Transphobia	The systemic oppression of transgender people because they do not fit society's expectations of what men and women are supposed to act and look like
Transsexual	A more clinical term that had historically been used to describe transgender people who sought medical intervention (eg, hormones or surgery) for gender affirmation. This term is less commonly used in the present day; however, some individuals and communities maintain a strong and affirmative connection to this term.
Two-spirit	A person, especially someone assigned male at birth, who adopts the gender identity, dress, and social roles traditionally assigned to a different gender. This can also be any of numerous culturally distinct genders apart from male or female, commonly among some Indigenous North American peoples.

Prevalence of Interpersonal Violence and IPV

As with other marginalized populations, it is difficult to determine the prevalence of interpersonal violence and IPV amongst the LGBTQIA+ population. Relationship violence is wrought with homophobia, biphobia, transphobia, heterosexism, and other forms of prejudice and oppression, such as sexism, racism, classism, and ableism.[1] Communities have dismissed LGBTQIA+ individuals' intimate relationships and experiences of victimization as marginal, unnatural, or insignificant.[5] There are only a handful of LGBTQIA+-specific interpersonal violence agencies in the United States. Furthermore, LGBTQIA+ victims of interpersonal violence may fear that disclosure of violence in same-sex relationships will add to the stereotypes that already exist in their community. They may fear that they are betraying the community and that they will lose some of the connections that are so important to their healing.[1] There is also a real concern that disclosure may be met with homophobic or transphobic responses by professionals they will interact with or friends and family that they may disclose to.[6] LGBTQIA+ individuals of color disproportionately experience violence. The violence they experience may involve not only their gender and sexuality but also may be based on their race.

Many large-scale studies on IPV do not include information from gay or lesbian individuals, nor do they consider the experiences of transgender, intersex, bisexual, or other queer people. Large-scale studies are flawed in that they rely on individuals self-selecting and self-reporting violence, but sometimes those individuals do not have the option to select the gender or identity that they identify with. In addition, these studies do not take into consideration the inconsistent language used to describe IPV, which may mean that an LGBTQIA+ woman may be reluctant to disclose sexual assault by another woman because the term "rape" is often perceived as only penile penetration. Because of these factors and others, most published statistics are likely to report low levels of violence. However, interpersonal violence in same-sex relationships is approximately the same rate as in heterosexual relationships and may be even higher (17% to 52%).[1]

As with other identities, research on bisexual individuals is also lacking. One study that did include bisexual as a category is the National Intimate Partner and Sexual Violence Survey in 2010. This study found that nearly 1 in 3 lesbian women and 1 in 2 bisexual women have experienced at least 1 form of severe physical violence by an intimate partner in her lifetime (compared to 1 in 4 heterosexual women) and the lifetime prevalence of rape, physical violence, and stalking by an intimate partner was 43.8% for lesbian women and 61.1% for bisexual women (compared to 35% for heterosexual women). For men, the lifetime prevalence of severe physical violence by an intimate partner is 16.4% for gay men and was unable to be determined for bisexual men because the numbers were too small to report (compared to 13.9% for heterosexual men). The lifetime prevalence of rape, physical violence, and/or stalking for gay men was 26%, and for bisexual men 37.3% (compared to heterosexual men at 29%).[7]

Few studies have been specifically conducted on people who identify as transgender or intersex. Of the studies that included transgender individuals, the median lifetime prevalence of physical IPV was 37.5% and the median lifetime prevalence of sexual IPV was 25%. Compared to cisgender people, transgender people were 1.7 times more likely to experience any IPV, 2.2 times more likely to experience physical IPV, and 2.5 times more likely to experience sexual IPV.[8] Another survey of transgender and intersex people found that 50% had been raped or assaulted by an intimate partner, yet only 62% of those raped or assaulted (31% of the total sample) identified as survivors of interpersonal violence when asked directly.[9] An additional consideration is that most of the research remains focused on White gay men and lesbians who are often in their mid-20s or 30s and college-educated,[1] so a lack of diversity can greatly affect the true reported incidence of IPV being experienced by the LGBTQIA+ community.

For a reliable source of information, the United States National Coalition of Anti-Violence Projects (NCAVP) releases an annual report, entitled *Lesbian, Gay, Bisexual, Transgender, Queer and HIV-Affected Hate and Intimate Partner Violence*.[10] This report looks at the experiences of survivors who reported to NCAVP member programs. In 2017, the NCAVP collected information on 2144 reports of IPV, a 6% increase from 2016. IPV survivors most commonly reported in-person verbal harassment (19%), physical violence (16%), threats and intimidation (11%), isolation (9%), harassment via a telephone or online (6%), and sexual violence (5%). For survivors of IPV, 48% sustained an injury, 45% reported seeking medical attention, and 23% reported that weapons were used during the incidents of violence. Cisgender men remain the largest group reporting IPV to NCAVP member organizations, and a majority of all IPV survivors identified as people of color. Transgender women who experienced IPV were nearly 2.5 times more likely to experience sexual violence and nearly 4 times more likely to experience financial abuse than survivors who did not identify as transgender women. Additionally, 44% of IPV survivors reported having a disability.

Complicating Factors and Obstacles to Accessing Supportive Services

When working with LGBTQIA+ survivors, it is important to acknowledge the complicating and marginalizing factors that a survivor may face, perhaps discouraging them from seeking or receiving appropriate services. Many LGBTQIA+ survivors lack access to safe spaces, competent resources, and social service providers who receive training specific to their needs.[2] Negative responses from crisis line workers, other social service providers, and law enforcement are well documented in the literature.[6] With heteronormative beliefs being so engrained in society, social service agencies may struggle to know which individual to support, believing that both partners are equally involved in violence. This belief can affect the mental health of the victim but also interfere with the legal system and other service providers responding appropriately.[2]

In interactions with law enforcement, more than 1/2 of LGBTQIA+ survivors report indifference or even hostility from police.[11] In states with mandatory arrest laws, police responding to LGBTQIA+ couples face challenges in identifying whom to arrest and are more likely to make a dual arrest when compared to heterosexual cases.[1] The power dynamics between the victim and perpetrator may be confusing, as they could be the same size and strength. Further, victims could use more physical violence as self-protection or to retaliate against the abuse; victims are thought to be passive, therefore, this may be confusing to responders.[1] Perpetrators are assumed to be more "masculine" or "butch" and victims are assumed to be more "femme," but this may not be the case.[1] These assumptions could ultimately lead to perpetrators ending up in shelters and community advocacy programs and survivors ending up in abuse intervention programs.[2]

An additional consideration is that since local safe spaces for the LGBTQIA+ community are often small and interconnected, the victim is likely to run into the person who abused them at community events or other shared community spaces. The abusive partner may have ways to get more information about the victim from other community members or look to ostracize the victim from the LGBTQIA+ community, further inhibiting the survivor from healing.[2]

The abuse may cause the victim to experience housing insecurity or even homelessness. According to the National LGBT Health Education Center, almost 1/2 of LGBTQIA+ survivors of abuse who seek shelter report being denied access; of those, nearly 1/3 are turned away because of their gender identity. Cisgender men and transgender people may have difficulty finding shelters that accommodate their gender. Survivors may also experience violence and discrimination in shelters. With the limited access to shelters and the abuser's desire to maintain power and control, the abusive same-gender partner may try to access the same shelter as the survivor, causing more harm.[11]

Many LGBTQIA+ individuals do not seek health care services, even when they need to, due to prior harmful and non-affirming experiences, discrimination, and costs, especially for intersex individuals. LGBTQIA+ individuals were more than 3 times as likely as non-LGBTQIA+ individuals to delay or avoid receiving needed medical care and preventative screenings because of disrespect or discrimination from a doctor or other health care provider. One-third of transgender or nonbinary respondents reported that they had to "teach their doctor or healthcare provider about transgender or nonbinary people in order to get appropriate care."[12]

Victims may also be reluctant to seek services from law enforcement, domestic violence shelters, and other service providers. 32% of LGBTQIA+ individuals–including 40% of LGBTQIA+ people of color and 55% of transgender and non-binary individuals–reported experiencing at least 1 negative experience or form of mistreatment when interacting with a mental health professional in the past year. 30% of LGBTQIA+ individuals and 51% of transgender or nonbinary individuals reported avoiding law enforcement to avoid experiences of discrimination based on their sexual orientation, gender identity, or sex characteristics.[12] All professionals should consider how their organization is ensuring that they are providing safe, affirming, and effective responses that look to decrease the impact that interpersonal violence has on an individual's health and recovery. Be aware that an abusive partner may present as a friend of a victim rather than an intimate partner and could compromise the abused individual's privacy and safety during provider interaction.[11]

Furthermore, organizations should implement implicit bias training as an annual requirement for all staff to help combat unrealized negative attitudes that staff have about the people they serve. If a service provider identifies as heterosexual, they may wrongly apply their heterosexual thinking to LGBTQIA+ relationships, creating a greater divide between the provider and the individual they are serving.

Types of Violence as Described in the Duluth Model

Abuse within a heterosexual relationship has been documented on the "Power and Control Wheel" developed in Duluth, Minnesota, and is also referred to as the "Duluth Model." The wheel has been adapted to show the different types of abuse that an LGBTQIA+ victim may experience. Below (in **Table 5-2**) is a summary of some of the common types of abuse seen amongst all victims of IPV and then types of abuse specifically related to the LGBTQIA+ population.

Table 5-2. A Comparison of Types of Abuse in Heterosexual and Non-Heterosexual Relationships[1,11,13,14]

Categories of Abuse	Common Among all Victims of IPV	Associated with LGBTQIA+
Physical	Hitting, punching, slapping, kicking, biting, restraining, pushing, strangling, bruises, broken bones, burns	Pulling hair; targeting a partner's genitals or chest; not letting a partner heal from gender-affirming surgery; denying a partner access to hormones; public displays of affection in dangerous (anti-LGBTQIA+) areas; withhold medication for HIV
Sexual	Forced sex, rape with an object or weapon, demeaning sexual comments	Damaging gender confirmation surgical tissue; using LGBTQIA+ stereotypes to coerce a partner into particular sex acts; saying that women cannot rape or men cannot be raped; using gender roles to control how a partner has sex; using words for a partner's body parts that do not align with their gender identity; forcing sex in exchange for necessities like food or housing; convincing a partner not to use sexual protection because "LGBTQIA+ sex is safer"
Emotional	Isolation, manipulation, humiliation, lying, threats to kill, threats to commit suicide, racial attacks, intimidation, depression, anger, shame, fear, suicidal ideation, post-traumatic stress	Intentionally using the wrong pronouns or name with a partner; damaging gender expression clothing or controlling how a partner expresses their gender or sexual orientation; stalking; saying no one will believe the victim because they are gay; accusing a partner of "mutual abuse"; saying women cannot abuse women; blaming the abuse on a partner's identity; denying abuse can exist in LGBTQIA+ communities; denying a partner's gender identity or sexual orientation; pressuring a partner to be "out" or "closeted"; defining abusive behaviors as a normal part of LGBTQIA+ relationships; turning mutual friends against a partner; using anti-LGBTQIA+ slurs or endorsing negative stereotypes; threats of suicide by the abusive partner; denying a partner access to LGBTQIA+ community supports and events
Verbal	Insults, name-calling, yelling	Threatening to "out" a partner to their family, work, or religious group; questioning if a partner is a "real" lesbian, "real" man, "real" woman, "real" femme, "real" butch, etc; reinforcing internalized homophobia; threats to reveal HIV/AIDS status; causing dramatic scenes at LGBTQIA+ events; convincing a partner that they will be rejected by others for their LGBTQIA+ identity; using anti-LGBTQIA+ discrimination to justify an "us against the world" mentality; using bi/trans/homophobia as an excuse to isolate a partner from others; threats to jeopardize immigration because of sexual orientation

(continued)

Table 5-2. A Comparison of Types of Abuse in Heterosexual and Non-Heterosexual Relationships[1,11,13,14] *(continued)*

Categories of Abuse	Common Among all Victims of IPV	Associated with LGBTQIA+
Financial	Creates debt, steals money, uses money to control another person	Damaging gender expression clothing; put assets in abusive partner's name only; threatening to out a partner at work; identity theft (easier when a partner is the same gender); demanding a partner pay for gender-affirming hormones or surgeries; using gender roles to demand a partner pays more

Case Studies

Case Study 5-1

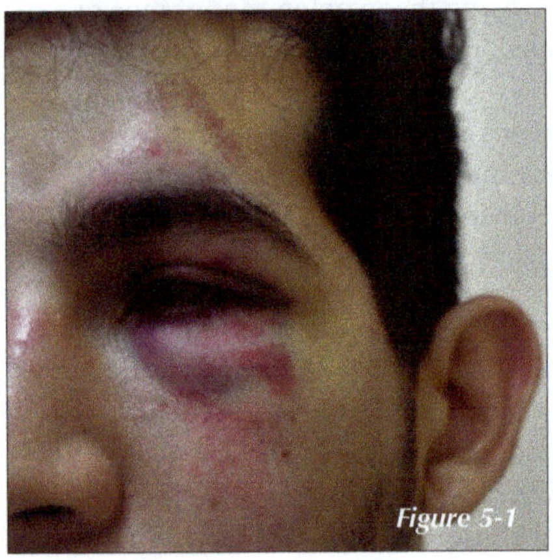

Figure 5-1. *Face injuries.*

Andre, a 21-year-old male trainer, was kicked out of his parents' house when he came out as gay a few years ago after he met Lewis, a 45-year-old male banker, and moved in with him. This was Andre's first gay relationship whereas Lewis was well established in the gay community. One night, Andre and Lewis went out with a group of Lewis's close friends to a dance club. When they got home, Andre told Lewis that he did not feel included. Lewis belittled Andre and said, "You just need to show up and look pretty. No one cares what you think." When Andre tried to walk away and ignore the comments, Lewis became angry. Lewis said, "You don't walk away from me. I give you everything, this house you live in, those expensive clothes you wear. If I want to yell at you, you will sit there and listen to it." Lewis then picked up a decorative vase and threw it at Andre, hitting him in the head. Andre felt dizzy, so he sat down on the couch. Lewis got into Andre's face, continued screaming and belittling him, and then punched him in the face multiple times. Andre just pretended to pass out so that Lewis would leave him alone. When Andre went to work the next day, his boss noticed the injuries (shown in **Figure 5-1**), asked Andre what happened, and then took Andre to the emergency department (ED). During the ED visit, Andre told the nurse that he did not have anyone to talk to about what happened, but he thought that Lewis was going to kill him because he was so angry.

Discussion

Andre was particularly vulnerable to experiencing interpersonal violence based on his age and being in his first same-sex relationship. During the assault, Andre experienced verbal harassment, physical violence, and isolation. With his boss's help, Andre could seek medical attention. The nurse established rapport, which allowed Andre to open up about what happened. The nurse should identify if there are LGBTQIA+-competent resources in the community that can support Andre. If Andre decides to leave, he may risk housing insecurity or homelessness as there are likely not any shelter beds available for him. Andre may decide to return to Lewis. Lewis is established in the gay community and Andre could be ostracized if he decides to make a police report or tell others about what happened. Lewis may have even told Andre that this is normal in gay relationships. The nurse should thoroughly document the injuries observed and statements made by Andre, provide him with resources for follow-up medical care and advocacy services, create a safety plan, and provide Andre with information about an order of protection. The nurse can tell Andre that physical violence and emotional abuse are not a natural or healthy part of any relationship, even a gay relationship. Ultimately, the nurse will need to trust Andre's decision regarding what is safest for him to do.

Case Study 5-2

LaTonya, a 23-year-old transgender female sex worker, was walking home after meeting up with a client when she was approached by Officer Jackson. He said he was concerned about LaTonya being on the street alone and offered to give her a ride. LaTonya knew that in exchange for the ride, she would be asked to perform oral sex on Officer Jackson. LaTonya did this willingly because she did not want to wait for the bus, and she was concerned that if she did not comply, then the officer would arrest her for sex work. When LaTonya got home, her new partner, James, asked how the night went. LaTonya told him that she got a ride home. James became upset and said, "I don't know why you go to work just to waste your money on a taxi." LaTonya disclosed that she got a free ride from a police officer who offered to help her, she just had to give him a blow job. James became even more upset, punched LaTonya in the face, and kicked her genitals multiple times causing LaTonya to fall. While LaTonya was lying on the ground, James kicked her in her chest and yelled, "How could you do that with the officer when you won't with me?"

LaTonya presented to the hospital the morning after the assault because she was having severe genital pain, chest pain, and facial pain from the assault. LaTonya told triage that she had difficulty urinating and could barely sit down because her genitals hurt so bad. LaTonya's medical record reflected her gender as male. LaTonya had been in the waiting room for 2 hours when she was finally brought back to the room, crying uncontrollably from the pain.

Discussion

A standard introduction with any victim/survivor should include name and pronouns, and ask them what name and pronouns they use. For example, "Hello. My name is Becca and I use she/her pronouns. I will be the advocate working with you today. What is your name and what pronouns do you use?" Normalizing the use of pronouns can help individuals feel more comfortable and in control when seeking services.

Transgender survivors like LaTonya may be reluctant to disclose previous medical information. Disclosing hormone therapy or previous surgeries could out them as being transgender. If there is someone else in the room who does not know they are transgender, this could be risky for them to discuss. Since LaTonya was kicked in the chest and genitals and is having pain, knowing about previous top or bottom surgery (ie, breast augmentation, silicone implants, vaginal reconstruction, vaginoplasty) would affect the possible injuries that she sustained from the assault. For any transgender survivor receiving services, they should know that they are in control of what happens during any exam of their body.

To provide services to LaTonya, her providers may need to do an anatomical (body part) inventory. If this is not necessary for services, then providers should not ask. A good way to approach this is to say, "To provide you with the best care, it would help me to know if you have certain body parts. Is it okay if we go through a list of body parts, and you can let me know whether you have these? If you use different words for parts of your body, please let me know." Using mirroring language will prevent providers from assuming that they know what is under someone's clothing. Using anatomical terms like "penis" or "vagina" could be traumatizing for someone who is transgender. It is important to implement non-gendered language into everyday conversations so that it is comfortable to do as part of care practice. Examples of this include using terms like chest/top, genitals/bottom, front hole, and back hole.

Summary

LGBTQIA+ survivors of interpersonal violence and IPV face many challenges in reporting to law enforcement, identifying and accessing resources, receiving medical care, and accessing mental health services. Professionals must remove these barriers so that LGBTQIA+ survivors can access resources without fear of disrespect or discrimination based on their sexual orientation, gender identity, or sex characteristics. Though this chapter focused specifically on LGBTQIA+ individuals, professionals must recognize other marginalized individuals in their communities who may face similar barriers to seeking services (eg, individuals with disabilities, military, and people of color). Professionals are responsible for having an awareness of evidence-based, trauma-informed, and victim-centered services and a desire to continue to seek out information, resources, consultation, and continuing education to enhance their provision of services.

Resources

LGBTQIA+-specific interpersonal violence and IPV resources[11]:

— Fenway Health Violence Recovery Program and Training: www.fenwayhealth.org/care/behavioral-health/violence-recovery

— FORGE: www.forge-forward.org

— National Coalition of Anti-Violence Programs: www.avp.org

— National LGBTQ Institute on IPV: www.LGBTQIPV.org

— The Network/La Red Hotline: 617.742.4911 www.TNLR.org

— The Northwest Network: www.nwnetwork.org

— Power and Control Wheel for LGBT Relationships

LGBTQIA+ health care training and education[11]:

— National LGBT Health Education Center: www.lgbthealtheducation.org

— Webinar: Implementing Routine Intimate Partner Violence Screening in a Primary Care Setting, www.lgbthealtheducation.org/webinar/lgbt-ipv-screening/

— Webinar: Intimate Partner Violence in LGBTQ communities, www.lgbthealtheducation.org/webinar/intimate-partner-violence-in-lgbtq-communities/

— Webinars and publications: Collecting sexual orientation and gender identity data, www.lgbthealtheducation.org/topic/sogi/

— Learning module: Providing Quality Care to Lesbian, Gay, Bisexual, and Transgender Patients: An Introduction for Staff Training, www.lgbthealtheducation.org/lgbt-education/learning-modules/

— Publication: Providing Inclusive Services and Care for LGBT People: A Guide for Health Care Staff, www.lgbthealtheducation.org/wp-content/uploads/Providing-Inclusive-Services-and-Care-for-LGBT-People.pdf

— Publication: Glossary of LGBT Terms for Health Care Teams, www.lgbthealtheducation.org/wp-content/uploads/2018/03/Glossary-2018-English-update-1.pdf

— Publication: Focus on Forms and Policy: Creating an Inclusive Environment for LGBT Patients, www.lgbthealtheducation.org/wp-content/uploads/2017/08/Forms-and-Policy-Brief.pdf

— Publication: Ten Things: Creating Inclusive Health Care Environments for LGBT People, www.lgbthealtheducation.org/wp-content/uploads/Ten-Things-Brief-Final-WEB.pdf

References

1. Ristock J, Timbang N. Relationship violence in lesbian/gay/bisexual/transgender/queer [LGBTQ] communities: moving beyond a gender-based framework. Violence Against Women Online Resources. 2005. https://citeseerx.ist.psu.edu/document?repid=rep1&type=pdf&doi=9a3abef3a779bf5911094e2075f565ed0b4870bb

2. Albright M, Alcantara-Thompson D. Contextualizing domestic violence from an lgbtq perspective. Northwest Network. 2011. Accessed February 2022. https://vawnet.org/material/contextualizing-domestic-violence-lgbtq-perspective

3. Mukerjee R, Wesp L, Singer R, Menkin D. *Clinician's Guide to LGBTQIA+ Care: Cultural Safety and Social Justice in Primary, Sexual, and Reproductive Healthcare*. Springer Publishing; 2021.

4. Dictionary.com. 2024. https://www.dictionary.com/

5. Beyond the wheel. The Northwest Network of Bisexual, Trans, Lesbian, and Gay Survivors of Abuse. 2009. Accessed February 2022. https://www.nwnetwork.org/

6. Brown M, Groscup J. Perceptions of same-sex domestic violence among crisis center staff. *J Fam Violence.* 2009;24:87-93. doi:10.1007/s10896-008-9212-5

7. Walters M, Chen J, Breiding M. *The National Intimate Partner and Sexual Violence Survey (NISVS): 2010 Findings on Victimization by Sexual Orientation*. National Center for Injury Prevention and Control, Centers for Disease Control and Prevention. 2013.

8. Peitzmeier SM, Malik M, Kattari SK, et al. Intimate partner violence in transgender populations: systematic review and meta-analysis of prevalence and correlates. *Am J Public Health.* 2020;110(9):e1-e14. doi:10.2105/AJPH.2020.305774

9. Courvant D, Cook-Daniels L. Trans and intersex survivors of domestic violence: defining terms, barriers, & responsibilities. National Coalition Against Domestic Violence. 2000. Accessed February 2022. https://vawnet.org/sites/default/files/materials/files/2016-08/TransandIntersexSurvivors.pdf

10. Tillery B, Ray A, Cruz E, Waters E. *Lesbian, Gay, Bisexual, Transgender, Queer and HIV-Affected Hate and Intimate Partner Violence in 2017*. The National Coalition of Anti-Violence Programs. 2017. Accessed February 2022. http://avp.org/wp-content/uploads/2019/01/NCAVP-HV-IPV-2017-report.pdf

11. National LGBT Health Education Center. *Recognizing and Addressing Intimate Partner Violence in Relationships of LGBTQ People: A Primer for Health Centers.* 2019. Accessed February 2024. https://www.lgbtqiahealtheducation.org/publication/recognizing-and-addressing-intimate-partner-violence-in-relationships-of-lgbtq-people-a-primer-for-health-centers/

12. Center for American Progress. *Discrimination and Barriers to Well-Being: The State of the LGBTQIA+ Community in 2022.* 2023. Accessed February 2024. https://www.americanprogress.org/article/discrimination-and-barriers-to-well-being-the-state-of-the-lgbtqi-community-in-2022/

13. The power and control wheel. Domestic Abuse Intervention Project. Accessed February 2022. https://www.thehotline.org/identify-abuse/power-and-control/

14. Lesbian/gay power and control wheel. National Center on Domestic and Sexual Violence. Accessed February 2022. https://www.familyjusticecenter.org/wp-content/uploads/2017/10/Lesbian-Gay-Power-_-Control-Wheel-Roe-_-Jagodinsky.pdf

Chapter 6

Domestic Violence in the Military Setting

Michelle Ortiz, MSN, RN, AFN-BC, SANE-A, IPVNE, SAMFE
Terri Augspurger, MSN, RN, AFN-BC, SANE-A, SANE-P
Amy Zabel, BSN, RN, SANE-A, RNC-MNN, IPVNE, LCDR, ANC

The views expressed in this chapter are those of the authors and do not necessarily reflect the official policy or position of the Department of the Navy, Department of Defense, or the United States Government.

Objectives

After reviewing this chapter, the reader will be able to:

1. *Outline risk factors for intimate partner violence (IPV).*
2. *List additional stressors unique to the military that increase the risk of IPV.*
3. *Discuss the legal system and processes specific to the military.*
4. *Define the Uniform Code of Military Justice.*
5. *Describe the differences between the civilian legal processes and the military legal processes.*
6. *Identify the resources and programs specific to the military created to prevent, decrease, and mitigate IPV.*

Introduction

Domestic violence (DV) is a serious public health issue that affects millions of Americans in both civilian and military communities. IPV, nearly synonymous with DV and being used in this chapter to refer to both terms, is defined as abuse or violence that occurs within a close relationship. The Centers for Disease Control and Prevention (CDC) defines DV as "physical violence, sexual violence, stalking, and psychological aggression (including coercive acts) by a current or former intimate partner."[1] Financial restraints and violence toward children and animals are also associated factors. The prevalence of IPV is multidimensional and difficult to effectively capture due to low reporting rates. The risk factors that present in civilian populations are numerous, and the same risk factors are often not only exemplified in the unique culture experienced by military personnel but also include factors exclusive to the military. This chapter will explore IPV as it is experienced and reported across all military branches and examine the preventive methods and resources that are currently in use or being developed to help protect service members and their families.

Risk Factors

It is well established in the literature that external and internal stressors may lead to an increased risk of IPV. Risk factors include gender, marital inequality, poverty, social exclusion, relationship contention, lack of familial support, and history of previous violence. The risks are applicable to all military populations including veterans, active-duty service members, and reservists. In addition to the risk factors mentioned, military members frequently experience additional stressful situations to which their civilian counterparts are not exposed. Many families' senses of safety and security are impacted by isolation and the absence of the support provided by extended family. Long deployments often subject members to violence and the horrors of war, and they are often abruptly returned to a completely different environment and a family unprepared for their presence. Negrusa & Negrusa[2] found that post-9/11 deployments adversely affected marital stability, citing combat-induced post-traumatic stress disorder (PTSD) as an important contributing factor. Later studies determined that spousal abuse is more common in military than civilian families.[3]

Prevalence

The true prevalence of IPV in the military is hard to determine, as identifying and tracking abuse in the military population can be difficult due to frequent relocations, poor continuity of case management, and ineffective follow-up. These challenges place military families at increased risk for continued abuse, long-term detrimental health outcomes, and homicide.

In the United States, "as many as 1 in 4 women and 1 in 9 men are victims of domestic violence."[4] Based on a thorough 2018 study,[5] it was determined that a significant percentage of both women and men, 36% and 34% respectively, have encountered physical violence, sexual violence, or stalking from an intimate partner at some point in their lives. The figures are particularly alarming for veterans and service members, with estimates indicating that the rates of such incidents could reach as high as 58% within these populations.[5] Furthermore, the data highlight a troubling trend among active-duty service members, who are reportedly 3 times more likely to engage in IPV compared to civilians.[5] The prevalence is likely significantly underreported due to some unique facets of military life:

— Many women forego coming forward to file a complaint for fear of getting their significant others in trouble with the military.

— If convicted of the abuse, the military member could be discharged from the military or have loss of a paygrade—both of which can impact the family's financial situation.

Barriers to Care

Women associated with the military, either as service members or dependents, are frequently physically, emotionally, psychologically, and financially abused. They often do not receive adequate interventions due to poor identification of red flags, lack of resources, and lack of reporting either by themselves or health care providers. Relocation also contributes to the lack of care, as moving every 2 to 3 years results in the loss of any support systems established in their current location. These frequent moves may also result in the loss of continuity in their medical records, which can lead to a lack of vital documentation in their medical history. For many years in the Department of Defense (DoD), not all service branches utilized the same electronic health record (EHR). Furthermore, even within the same system, each type of visit might be categorized differently from branch to branch. Outpatient visits were historically recorded under one EHR, while emergency department (ED) visits and inpatient encounters had their own systems. Victims may also visit civilian hospitals and clinics, rendering them "invisible" to the military health care system. Due to these differences in locations, there has been a lack in communication. Fortunately, this disparity has been recognized, and the slow consolidation into communicating programs or 1 universal program is in progress.

Legal System

Members of the military are required to abide by the laws of the United States (as well as host countries' laws while deployed/stationed overseas), but they must also obey another set of laws unique to the military. These laws, known as The Uniform Code of Military Justice (UCMJ), were created specifically for the military. The UCMJ is a group of articles in federal law that is applicable to all active-duty personnel, reservists, and National Guardsmen.[6] While the names and numbers that represent the offenses covered in the UCMJ are different, the offenses do correlate to many State and Federal statutes.

The current process for moving forward with charges in an alleged sexual assault or battery case is also unique to the military. Sexual assault goes hand-in-hand with IPV; they are often referred to as sister crimes, as these cases regularly include components of sexual battery or assault. For unrestricted sexual assault reports, the Command of the accused is notified when the victim discloses violence. Then, once the investigation has concluded, the resulting information is presented to the Command of the accused for the decision to move to prosecution.[7] For many years, this process has received much scrutiny. Recently, Congress passed legislation to take the process out of the hands of the military chain of command and instead use an independent counsel's office that will be established to oversee the cases.[8] Currently, this modification applies only to cases involving sexual assault or battery. However, with increased awareness and positive outcomes, the expectation is that changes to the IPV process will follow.

Interventions and Resources

Forensic Health Care Examiners

The Defense Health Agency (DHA) combines all the branches of military medicine into a single entity with the intent of universal consistency and standardization of protocols and procedures governing military medical care. A specific intention of the DHA is to eventually transform the Sexual Assault Military Forensic Examiner (SAMFE) position into comprehensive Forensic Health Examiners (FHE), allowing any examiner to care for all types of assault. Consequently, this transformation will potentially improve conviction rates in the DoD, as currently not all programs offer forensic exams to patients who do not fit the sexual assault criteria. FHEs collect samples with the intent of preservation and protection for future use in the judicial system.

Along with potential evidentiary samples that may be analyzed and utilized in court proceedings, photo documentation of the patient's injuries at presentation is an option. Of equal importance, the documentation of the patient's history of abuse creates a record for tracking incidents and possible presentation in court martial. Per the DoD's Fiscal Year 2019 Annual Report on Sexual Assault,[9] of the 795 sexual assault cases that went to court, 73% of them resulted in a conviction of at least 1 charge at trial. Additional data regarding the DoD's report can be found in **Table 6-1** and **Figure 6-1**.

Currently, in some medical treatment facilities (MTFs), IPV patients are being cared for by emergency room (ER) physicians and staff instead of FHEs. Future goals include a forensic examiner in every military hospital that has a 24/7 ER, decreased recurring incidents of abuse in families affiliated with the military, and programs that teach all military members to recognize abuse and how to access resources for these patients and themselves. Having forensic examiners care for all IPV patients ensures proper training and standardization of services offered regardless of what MTF to which they report.

Table 6-1. Reports and Incidents of Spouse Abuse (FY 2011-FY 2020)[9]

Fiscal Year (FY)	Reported Incidents	Met Criteria Incidents	Married Couples Population	Reports /1000	Met Criteria Incidents/1000
2011	19 277	8386	753 110	25.6	11.1
2012	18 671	8345	734 308	25.4	11.4
2013	17 295	7935	713 135	24.3	11.1
2014	16 287	7464	690 460	23.6	10.8
2015	15 725	7892	665 429	23.6	11.9
2016	15 144	7661	646 782	23.4	11.8
2017	15 657	7153	638 132	24.5	11.2
2018	15 242	7015	628 167	24.3	11.2
2019	13 571	6800	626 705	21.7	10.9
2020	12 663	6596	620 387	20.4	10.6

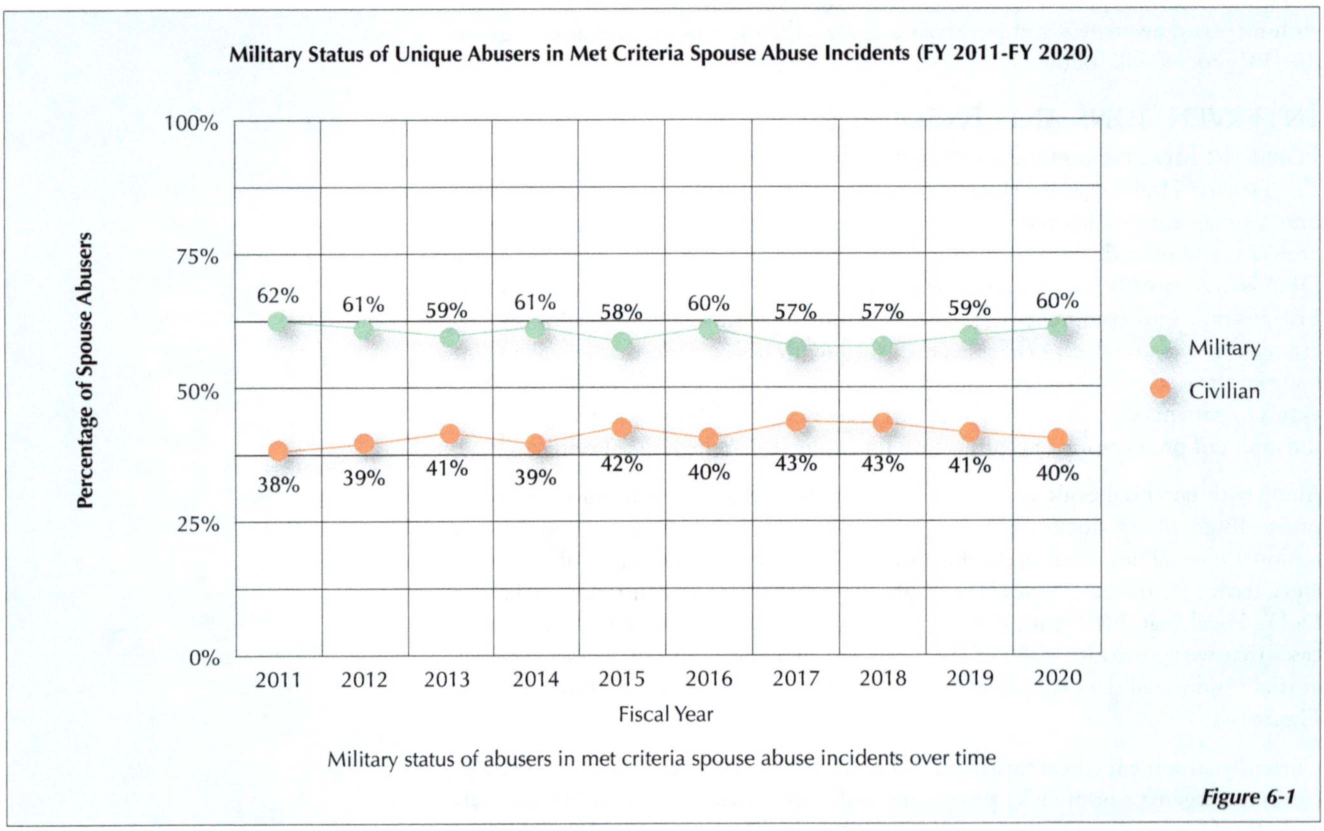

Figure 6-1. *Military Status of Unique Abusers in Met Criteria Spouse Abuse Incidents (FY 2011-FY 2020).*[9]

According to the World Health Organization, studies conducted around the world showed that 40% to 70% of female murder victims were killed by their husband or boyfriend.[10] Because of the incidence and severity of IPV, the International Association of Forensic Nurses and the Emergency Nurses Association partnered to issue a joint statement saying that all nurses should routinely screen patients for IPV, and forensic nurses should be helping with the care of these vulnerable patients.[11] Many civilian hospitals have recognized the value and benefits of having sexual assault nurse examiners (SANEs) care for IPV patients, and the military is slowly making the transition to this system. The current DoD instruction outlines the training of SANEs and mandates that all military hospitals with a 24/7 ER have a forensic program. The proposed DHA instruction will require EDs to begin incorporating all components of forensic examinations into offered services, including sexual assault, domestic violence (inclusive of strangulation encounters), and eventually pediatric maltreatment (on a limited basis). The intent is to provide standardization of policies along with enhanced screening and care for all military beneficiaries.

Suspect Exams

The military instructions also afford for examination and treatment of suspects, which differs from the civilian sector. FHEs are trained to care for all parties involved in IPV, and this process allows for the potential recovery of valuable evidence from both the victim and suspect. The flexibility to provide both types of examinations demonstrates the impartiality of the FHE in the medical forensic examination process and thus guards the question of bias in court martial proceedings.

Family Advocacy Program Initiation

As previously discussed, military service at its most basic level involves substantial occupational stressors for members, which can extend into their families as well. Consequently, policymakers have rightfully identified this group as a vulnerable population. In 1981, the DoD implemented a directive[12] that requires each branch of the US Armed Forces to implement the Family Advocacy Program (FAP) to address and prevent child maltreatment and spousal abuse. It also established a confidential registry to collect and analyze data associated with its services.[9] All incidents of suspected child maltreatment or spousal abuse in military families are referred to the FAP, where a case review committee, composed of a multidisciplinary team of designated individuals working at the military instillation level, is tasked with the evaluation and determination of abuse or neglect. The team also develops and coordinates the treatment and disposition recommendations for the abused member. As DV continues to be an issue affecting military families, another DoD instruction was implemented in August 2007. The Domestic Abuse Involving DoD Military and Certain Affiliated Personnel Instruction was designed to "prevent and eliminate domestic abuse in the Department of Defense" and "provide for the safety of victims; hold abusers appropriately accountable for their behavior; and coordinate the response to domestic abuse with the local community."[13] In addition to the FAP, system-wide educational interventions are needed. Such educational interventions would include educating military members about the warning signs of DV so that it can be reported to the chain of command for awareness, intervention, and response; training SANEs to care for and document the stories and injuries associated with military IPV patients; and instituting suspected IPV measures within the hospital, including full medical work up and appropriate testing procedures.

Training: Reporting Options and Awareness Programs

There is an ongoing need for training within the military regarding the reporting options victims of DV have. All branches do receive annual, primarily computer-based training about DV, IPV, child abuse, the FAP, and the Sexual Assault Prevention and Response program, and how to access resources. However, more training beyond the required minimum can ensure as many members as possible have the broadest scope of actionable knowledge. Per the FAP instruction, adults can report DV to medical professionals and receive either a restricted or unrestricted report. With an unrestricted report, law enforcement is notified, and an investigation is started in addition to the medical care the victim receives. In a restricted report, the victim is eligible for medical care, but the report is not sent to law enforcement for investigation. Some military members and dependents do not know that a restricted report is an option, but with more education and information about the different types of reporting, more victims may come forward for treatment. Because of these unique stressors to both the military member and their families, more resources need to be implemented to help the active-duty member transition back into the family environment after deployments.

The FAP helps not only the victims when they are identified, but it also offers many programs to help decrease the incidence of DV at the source. Some of these programs include marriage counseling, new parent support programs, and financial counseling. However, many of these programs are underutilized, as much of the military population is not aware of all the programs that are offered. Better education of their existence and accessibility could help prevent violence in the future.

Health Records

Instituting an EHR that all military providers have access to for all patients regardless of duty station or where they were previously treated would be beneficial for identifying and tracking abuse. The Federal Electronic Health Record Modernization (FEHRM) Program Office's primary mission is to implement a single, common EHR.[14] There has been some progress, as in April 2020, FEHRM launched a joint health information exchange known as MHS Genesis, which connects providers in the private sector who are willing to share clinical information with the DoD and Veterans Affairs providers. This network allows military providers access to the records of military patients who may have been seen in the private sector. The Defense Health Agency-Interim Procedures Memorandum 19-004 established the procedures and timeline for implementing MHS Genesis at all military medical facilities.[14] MHS Genesis will be able to integrate both inpatient and outpatient visits into a single record system that will be accessible at all military installations and routine care facilities.

Currently, the military has a standardized form that is used to care for sexual assault patients. If a sexual assault patient reports to a military provider for medico-legal forensic care and requests a sexual assault forensic exam (SAFE), the FHE would fill out DD form 2911. This form is used by all SAMFEs to document the patient's consent, medical and assault history, physical exam, photographs taken, and any samples obtained. Having standardized documentation would make the exam more easily recognizable in a court of law and by other medical examiners.

Victim's Legal Counsel and Special Victims Counsel

The Victim's Legal Counsel (VLC), also referred to as the Special Victims' Counsel (SVC), is a unique service provided by the military system. In the judicial system, this specialized group is comprised of attorneys who represent individual victims and assist with the legal and administrative processes involved in filing a report.[7] These designated attorneys are part of an independent chain of command, uninfluenced by the commands affiliated with the victim, the alleged offender, the prosecution, and defense teams. Eligible victims (eg, active-duty, reservists, and dependents, including spouses and children) are entitled to legal counsel, free of charge, at any time during the case.[7] VLC/SVCs are governed by separate instruction.

There are many benefits to utilizing the VLC, including assistance with navigating the military justice system, guidance in general legal matters, and administrative challenges. The legal counsel will work with the victim advocates, FAP, trial counsel, forensic examiners, and the convening authority to ensure the reporting victim's rights are upheld. Legal counsel presence can lead to more effective and efficient interviews of the victim, while ensuring that their rights are observed and their interests are represented.[7] Importantly, this team affords a "voice and a choice,"[7] allowing the victim the option to participate in the process or to simply decline.

Case Study

Case Study 6-1

A 35-year-old female presented to the military base emergency center with an initial complaint of uterine contractions. She was pregnant at 27-weeks' gestation, gravida 3, para 2, with her third child and had a history of pre-term contractions with spotting of blood. On intake, she disclosed that she had fallen onto her side and subsequently began to feel contractions. She was accompanied by her spouse, who was the father of her unborn child. The patient was transferred to the OB/GYN department's perinatal unit for fetal monitoring.

Upon intake on the unit, the provider asked the spouse to leave the room to elicit patient history. The patient was attached to the fetal monitor, which indicated she was having irregular contractions. The provider observed that the patient was distressed, and upon further questioning about the reported fall, she disclosed a violent encounter that included nonfatal strangulation attempts and forced sexual acts. The spouse was an active-duty military member, and upon realizing that the staff was now possibly aware of an alleged assault, he fled the floor and hospital campus. The provider activated the FHE team, who responded to the unit.

Discussion

During the SAFE intake process, the patient requested a restricted report. However, the serious medical situation and threat to the patient and her unborn child, combined with the imminent danger reported, necessitated a report to federal law enforcement. The requirement for mandatory reporting was explained to the patient, and she was assured that the sexual components would be omitted from the report to accommodate her wishes. The amount of detail provided to investigators would remain at her discretion. Notifications were made to the following: federal law enforcement, sexual assault response coordinators, victim advocates, and hospital security. Hospital security secured the unit and began the task of locating the spouse to assure safety of all patients, staff, etc. Investigators responded, both federal and local, as the jurisdiction occurred at a family residence within local authority jurisdiction. Federal law enforcement remained on-site to assure safety and coordinate with local authorities. The teams were briefed on the status of the patient and requested that all interview processes be delayed due to the instability of the situation. Two FHEs responded, one of whom was solicited specifically due to the specialty of nurse midwifery. This allowed for interpretation of the fetal monitoring to ensure patient and fetal stability throughout the medical forensic examination process.

The patient reported 3 separate strangulation attempts over the previous 3 days. Two of the incidents resulted in loss or near loss of consciousness and 1 included the loss of urinary continence. An order was submitted for a computed tomography angiography, and the examiners accompanied the patient to radiology since consent for the medical forensic examination was obtained. Upon return from radiology, the exam resumed, and multiple injuries were noted and photo documented. Of note were the superficial injuries to the anterior and posterior neck. An alternate light source (ALS) was utilized, and contrast was noted in oval shapes, consistent with fingertip bruising. Additionally, a crescent shaped laceration was delineated with a yellow lens utilized on the ALS. The examination also revealed palpable tenderness and decreased range of neck motion. The examiners collaborated with local law enforcement to exchange photo documentation and decrease the patient's stress. Arrangements for extensive "observation" status were made due to the lack of availability for a safe harbor for the patient.

The spouse was located within 48 hours and hospitalized due to suicidal ideation, and he was subsequently detained due to the severity of charges. The patient was eventually discharged and relocated with family several states away. Her labor was delayed; however, the baby was still premature at 32 weeks and had some health anomalies that may have been attributed to intra-uterine anoxia, prematurity, or maternal stress.

The patient decided to change the status of the report to unrestricted/investigatory the evening she presented to the ER, and a full investigation ensued into both the DV and concurrent sexual battery. The medical documentation and photo documentation, including the ALS pictures, played an important role in the case as the spouse denied compression to the neck. Swabs from the anterior and posterior neck tested positive for epithelial DNA, as did swabs from the patient's necklace. This evidence, coupled with the ALS pictures revealing multiple oval-shaped contrasts (consistent with fingers, the method of strangulation reported by the patient), further supported the patient's case and led the examiners to thoroughly examine the areas of trauma reported.

The case was scheduled to go to trial, but after several negotiations, a plea was agreed upon. The examiners were asked to testify at the sentencing hearing, and the feedback from legal was that the testimony proved valuable to panel that determined the ultimate sentence. The spouse received jail time, a dishonorable discharge, and was required to register as a sexual offender.

The outcome in this case is fortunate in that the mother and baby survived, and timely response from responders mitigated the situation. However, the situation escalated to the point of injury, with long-lasting consequences for both parties. It is worth noting that the offending spouse had a medical record with a diagnosis for untreated PTSD, and services to assist with adjustment and concurrent life stressors were not sought. This lack of treatment and assistance with the adjustment and concurrent family and life stressors undoubtedly played a role in his perpetration of abuse.

Summary

DV is a global health issue that affects more than just the military community. However, because of the multiple challenges of the military setting, this population is at greater risk. Constant moves, uprooting from support systems, and separation from family are continual additional stressors on military families. Factor in multiple deployments in often violent or non-hospitable settings over a career, and the risks are accentuated. When the service member returns from deployment, it is not just an adjustment period for the military member, but also the family unit. Increasing the availability of education regarding current programs will increase their utilization and preventable measures. Implementing the use of forensic examiners on abuse cases to include DV and IPV will increase the identification of DV cases and standardize care across the DoD enterprise. This will help care for patients and hopefully result in greater conviction rates across the DoD. Changes in judicial processes that hold perpetrators accountable will potentially lead to fewer incidents and decrease negative patient outcomes.

References

1. Niolon PH, Kearns M, Dills J, et al. Prevent intimate partner violence across your lifespan. Centers for Disease Control and Prevention. 2017. Acessed December 20, 2021. https://www.cdc.gov/violence-prevention/media/pdf/resources-for-action/IPV-Prevention-Resource_508.pdf

2. Negrusa B, Negrusa S. Home front: post deployment mental health and divorces. *Demography.* 2014;51(3)895-916. doi:10.1007/s13524-014-0294-9

3. Cesur R, Sabia J. When war comes home: the effect of combat service on domestic violence. *Rev Econ Stat.* 2016;98(2):209-225. doi:10.1162/REST_a_00541

4. Huecker M, King KC, Jordan GA, Smock W. *Domestic Violence.* StatPearls; 2022. https://www.ncbi.nlm.nih.gov/books/NBK499891/

5. Cowlishaw S, Freijah I, Kartal D, et al. Intimate partner violence (IPV) in military and veteran populations: a systematic review of population-based surveys and population screening studies. *Int J Environ Res Public Health.* 2022;19(14):8853. doi:10.3390/ijerph19148853

6. Absher J. The Uniform Code of Military Justice (UCMJ). Military.com. March 25, 2022. Accessed April 5, 2022. https://www.military.com/join-armed-forces/the-uniform-code-of-military-justice-ucmj.html

7. Jones ML, CAPT, USN, JAGC. Interacting with the victim's legal counsel. VLC Brief. Accessed April 5, 2022. https://www.jag.navy.mil/legal-services/vlc/

8. Shane L III. Major overhaul in how the military handles sexual misconduct cases may finally happen. Military Times. April 29, 2021. Accessed April 5, 2022. https://www.militarytimes.com/news/pentagon-congress/2021/04/29/major-overhaul-in-how-the-military-handles-sexual-misconduct-cases-may-finally-happen/

9. Department of Defense Annual Report on Sexual Assault in the Military Fiscal Year 2019. US Department of Defense. April 28, 2020. Accessed April 15, 2022. https://www.defense.gov/News/Releases/Release/Article/2170913/department-of-defense-releases-fiscal-year-2019-annual-report-on-sexual-assault/

10. Violence against women. World Health Organization. March 9, 2021. Accessed December 4, 2021. https://www.who.int/en/news-room/fact-sheets/detail/violence-against-women

11. Domestic violence examiner: DV/IPV is a health issue. International Association of Forensic Nurses. Accessed August 1, 2022. https://static1.squarespace.com/static/53e530a1e4b021a99e4dc012/t/54d91c78e4b0e5cfc4424aad/1423514744544/Intimate_Partner_Violence_Nu.pdf

12. DoD Instruction 6400.01: Family Advocacy Program (FAP). May 1, 2019. Accessed December 1, 2021. https://www.esd.whs.mil/Portals/54/Documents/DD/issuances/dodi/640001p.pdf?ver=2019-05-01-081705-580

13. DoD Instruction 6400.06: DoD coordinated community response to domestic abuse involving DoD military and certain affiliated personnel. Updated May 10, 2022. Accessed June 28, 2022. https://www.esd.whs.mil/Portals/54/Documents/DD/issuances/dodi/640006p.pdf

14. Electronic Health Record: MHS Genesis. The Military Health System. Updated June 8, 2022. Accessed June 28, 2022. https://www.health.mil/Military-Health-Topics/MHS-Transformation/MHS-GENESIS

Chapter 7

Identification and Response to Interpersonal Violence in the Health Care Setting

Kate Lawler, MPH

Objectives

After reviewing this chapter, the reader will be able to:

1. *Identify the opportunities and challenges of addressing interpersonal violence in a health care setting.*
2. *Describe the benefits of an advocate agency colocating within a health care setting.*
3. *Understand, through case demonstrations, how to best identify and respond to interpersonal violence within a health care setting.*

Introduction

As contradictory as it may sound, most health care providers are both well-positioned and ill-equipped to address interpersonal violence. Health care providers are in an ideal position to address interpersonal violence because they see a high volume of patients each day, often have a reason to talk with patients alone, and are entrusted with sensitive information that may signal "red flags." However, health care providers face tremendous pressures on their time, which can limit their capacity to address interpersonal violence. This limitation may be less challenging, though, in a hospital setting that has multidisciplinary teams, including allied professionals such as social workers, who are charged with crisis intervention and discharge planning. Most ambulatory settings, however, do not have the benefit of having these allied professionals embedded on-site, usually due to a lack of insurance reimbursement or other resources to fund these positions. In both acute and ambulatory settings, partnerships with community-based domestic violence organizations can complement the existing health care provider's expertise, cultural and language capacity, services, and resources.

Definition and Statistics

Interpersonal violence refers to physical violence, sexual violence, stalking, or psychological harm by one person to another person that they have a personal relationship with. This type of violence can occur among heterosexual or same-sex couples as well as families, friends, or roommates. Some programs that support survivors of interpersonal violence also include abuse by in-laws among the forms of harm they address.[1]

Figure 7-1 illustrates how prevalent interpersonal violence is among both adult women and men. Interpersonal violence is also common among adolescents. Almost 1 in 11 female teenagers and 1 in 14 male teenagers report having experienced

Interpersonal Violence Prevalence

— About 1 in 5 women and about 1 in 7 men report having experienced severe physical violence from an intimate partner in their lifetime.

— About 1 in 5 women and about 1 in 12 men report having experienced contact sexual violence by an intimate partner.

— 10% of women and 2% of men report having been stalked by an intimate partner.

Figure 7-1

***Figure 7-1.**[2] Interpersonal violence prevalence.*

physical dating violence in the last year.[3] Applying these figures to 2020 United States Census data for 10 to 19 year olds, this would mean that nearly 2 million female teenagers and 1.5 million male teenagers report physical dating violence in a year.[4]

Screening

Evidence regarding the benefits of screening for interpersonal violence in the health care setting is mixed. The United States Preventive Services Task Force, an independent volunteer panel of national experts in prevention and evidence-based medicine, has given a B grade (on a scale of A, B, C, D, I [Insufficient Evidence]) to its recommendation that clinicians should screen for interpersonal violence in women of reproductive age.[5] The studies that this recommendation were based on found a wide range in the sensitivity and specificity of interpersonal violence screening instruments used in health care settings; therefore, there is not a lot of certainty as to whether patient responses to screening questions asked in a health care setting actually reflect the patient's experience. This may be due to patients not disclosing their interpersonal violence experiences for a variety of reasons. Patients may be afraid that child welfare authorities will be called, or they may have fears related to their immigration status or sexual orientation. Patients may also fear that the health care system's response to their disclosure will put them in greater danger (eg, the police confronting their abuser, but not yet being able to offer long-term protection for them). Leaving or attempting to leave an abusive partner can be more dangerous than staying. Studies have found that leaving an abusive partner is associated with a higher risk of homicide.[6] It is important for providers to understand this level of danger, first so that they do not pressure survivors to leave and second, so that programs are offering safety resources to patients who will be returning to the abusive situation.

In addition to the hesitation that survivors may feel about disclosing any abuse to a screening question within a health care setting, health care providers often face their own set of barriers in asking the screening questions. In particular, providers have cited a lack of training, protocols, or referral mechanisms as reasons that they do not feel fully prepared to screen patients for interpersonal violence.[7]

While interpersonal violence screening effectiveness is still relatively unproven, best practice guidelines do exist for helping health care providers avoid factors that are likely to create barriers to disclosure. Some of these best practices include building rapport with the patient before asking any screening questions, stating limits to confidentiality in advance, asking screening questions when the patient is alone, only using professional interpreters (rather than family or friends) if the patient speaks a different language, and using a framing statement.[8]

Universal Education

Given that many people who report not experiencing interpersonal violence when asked the screening questions actually are experiencing harmful relationships, universal education provides an opportunity for patients to access information on interpersonal violence resources regardless of whether or not they disclosed their abuse. Universal education usually involves a short statement by a health care provider such as, "Since we know that harmful or stressful relationships can affect our health, we provide information to all of our patients about where they can get support if this kind of relationship is happening to you or a friend." The provider should then give the patient a brochure with phone numbers and websites of interpersonal violence organizations to look at in the moment or to take home, if it is safe to do so (**Table 7-1**). Signage in restrooms and other places around the health care setting is another form of universal education for staff and patients alike.

Table 7-1. Interpersonal Violence Organizations

Organization	Website	Contact Information
National Domestic Violence Hotline	www.ndvh.org	Hotline: 1-800-799-7233 TTY: 1-800-787-3224 Text: Start to 88788
National Sexual Assault Hotline	www.rainn.org	Hotline: 1-800-656-4673
Love Is Respect	www.loveisrespect.org	Hotline: 1-866-331-9474 TTY: 1-866-331-8453 Text: loveis to 22522
National Human Trafficking Hotline	https://humantraffickinghotline.org/	Hotline: 1-888-373-7888 Text: HELP or INFO to 233733

Trauma-Informed Care

Another best practice that can positively impact patients regardless of whether they disclose their abuse is trauma-informed care. The Substance Abuse and Mental Health Services Administration (SAMHSA) defines trauma-informed care as one that realizes the widespread impact of trauma and understands potential paths for recovery; recognizes the signs and symptoms of trauma in clients, families, staff, and others involved with the system; responds by fully integrating knowledge about trauma into policies, procedures, and practices; and seeks to actively resist retraumatization.[9] The chart below outlines the 6 guiding principles of a trauma-informed approach (**Figure 7-2**). Part of a trauma-informed approach to interpersonal violence is understanding that it occurs in all socioeconomic groups and across all genders and sexual orientations.

Colocation of Domestic Violence Organizations

To better serve survivors of abuse, the out-stationing of domestic violence agency staff into health care settings combines the strengths of both institutions. As mentioned previously, health care providers see a high volume of patients in settings that typically involve confidential conversations, yet they often lack the time to take advantage of the opportunity to intervene. Domestic violence agency staff, on the other hand, are trained for and do have the time to sit with survivors for crisis intervention, safety planning, explanation of options, and counseling. However, they usually work in undisclosed locations without access to the broader public. When domestic violence agency staff are colocated within health care settings, they can

Six Guiding Principles to a Trauma-Informed Approach

The Centers for Disease Control and Prevention's (CDC) Office of Public Health Preparedness and Response (OPHPR), in collaboration with SAMHSA's National Center for Trauma-Informed Care (NCTIC), developed and led a new training for OPHPR employees about the role of trauma-informed care during public health emergencies. The training aimed to increase responder awareness of the impact that trauma can have in the communities where they work. Participants learned SAMHSA's six principles that guide a trauma-informed approach, including:

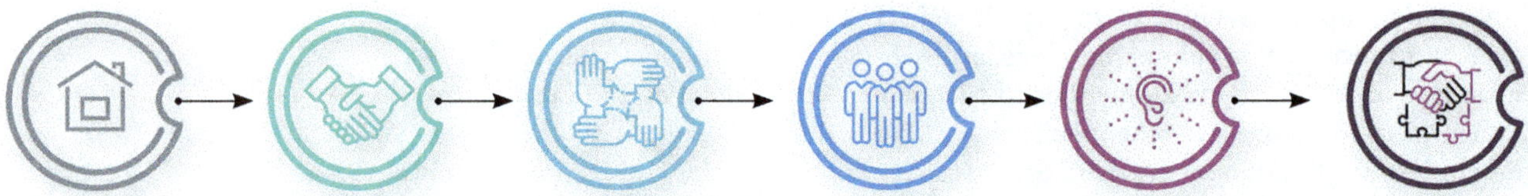

1. Safety
2. Trustworthiness and Transparency
3. Peer Support
4. Collaboration and Mutuality
5. Empowerment, Voice, and Choice
6. Cultural, Historical, and Gender Issues

Adopting a trauma-informed approach is not accomplished through any single particular technique or checklist. It requires constant attention, caring awareness, sensitivity, and possibly a cultural change at an organizational level. Ongoing internal organizational assessment and quality improvement, as well as engagement with community stakeholders, will help to embed this approach which can be augmented with organizational development and practice improvement. The training provided by OPHPR and NCTIC was the first step for the CDC to view emergency preparedness and response through a trauma-informed lens.

Figure 7-2

Figure 7-2.[10] *Six Guiding Principles to a Trauma-Informed Approach.*

engage in training with the hospital staff, meet with patients at bedside for crisis intervention and safety planning, and follow up with patients for case management and counseling. The health care setting often provides a safe "cover" for follow-up appointments if an abuser is tracking or controlling the survivor's movements because these meetings can occur under the guise of medical appointments. The colocation of domestic violence organizations in health care settings also requires that policies and procedures are set in place to ensure that both institutions are fulfilling their obligations to protect the confidentiality of a patient's information.

Case Studies

Case Study 7-1

Sudha was an Urdu-speaking patient in the mother-baby unit of an urban hospital in the United States. The nurse caring for Sudha needed to give a postpartum assessment that included 2 screening questions related to interpersonal violence. However, whenever the nurse went into the patient's room, several family members were present. At one point, the nurse found the patient alone with an older woman who looked like she might be the patient's mother. Since the patient's husband was not present, the nurse thought it might be a good opportunity to ask the screening questions, but she remembered that the training emphasized the patient being alone. When the nurse saw the older woman leave the room, she then returned to the patient's room to ask the screening questions via a phone interpreter. The nurse used a framing statement before asking the questions, saying, "We know that many of our patients are in relationships with someone who is hurting or controlling them. Therefore, we ask some questions to all of our patients when they are alone. Is it okay if I ask you these questions?" From the patient's answers, the nurse learned that the patient lived with her husband and in-laws. While her husband was sometimes verbally abusive, the most severe mistreatment came from her mother-in-law, who had just left the room.

Discussion

This case emphasizes the importance of the best practice guidelines. There are many reasons why a patient may not want to answer the screening questions in front of another person, particularly if that person is the perpetrator or if they are involved in their harm in any way. For similar reasons, family members may not be reliable language interpreters, thus a third party should always be used during the screening process. Additionally, since the nurse mentioned that she asks every patient the same questions in her framing statement, she helped the patient feel that she was not being singled out.

Case Study 7-2

Carla was a survivor of interpersonal violence and sexual abuse who recently had her second baby. During the postpartum hospital stay with her first child, Carla was retraumatized by the many nurses who were coming into her room and lifting up her shirt to try to help her breastfeed. This was triggering for Carla because it mimicked the loss of control over her body that she had experienced as part of her abuse.

The hospital where she had her second baby, however, had staff who was trained by the guiding principles of trauma-informed care. These nurses created a sense of safety and trust before they physically assisted Carla with breastfeeding. Furthermore, they asked for permission before touching Carla, explained step-by-step what they would do ahead of time, and empowered her with choices and the ability to stop at any time.

Discussion

Because 1 in 5 women experience physical violence from an intimate partner in their lifetime,[3] it is likely that a similar proportion of female staff and patients in a health care setting have had these experiences as well and should be mindful of this while treating patients. In the case above, neither the first nor second hospital were aware of Carla's history of abuse. If the first hospital had been aware, they more than likely would have taken more time to make her feel comfortable and safe with her first breastfeeding experience. By infusing trauma-informed principles into the health care setting, however, the second hospital was effectively using universal practices by assuming that all patients have experienced trauma. These practices make patients like Carla feel safe whether or not they have disclosed their abuse.

Case Study 7-3

Lyle came to the emergency department (ED) of an urban hospital for a head injury following an abusive incident with his boyfriend. His nurse explained that the hospital partners with an agency that helps people who are in relationships with someone who hurts or scares them. She asked Lyle if he would like to meet with a domestic violence advocate who could provide resources and talk with him about staying safe. Lyle consented to a meeting in the ED with the advocate. The advocate discussed the services of her organization with Lyle, provided him with a burner phone to stay in touch with her, and organized a ride for Lyle to his friend's house. The next week, Lyle and the advocate met in her outpatient office on the hospital's campus for ongoing counseling and case management.

Discussion

Lyle is an example of a patient who likely would not have come into contact with the services of a domestic violence organization without the colocation arrangement within the hospital. The ED provided the setting for a confidential conversation, during which the advocate was able to build trust and rapport. The nurse carefully explained the option of having the advocate visit his room so that Lyle could give informed consent. The advocate's office on the hospital campus provided a way for Lyle to continue receiving services and support without raising suspicion from his boyfriend.

Summary

Interpersonal violence is a prevalent issue that has an impact on physical and mental health. Health care settings can address this important health issue through training, screening and response protocols, a trauma-informed culture, and by partnering with domestic violence organizations. People in health care can offer assistance, resources, and empathy to those who need it. It is impossible to force people to accept help, but health care professionals can help establish building blocks of trust and support.

References

1. Intimate partner violence. Centers for Disease Control and Prevention. Updated October 2020. Accessed September 19, 2021. https://www.cdc.gov/violenceprevention/intimatepartnerviolence/index.html

2. Basile KC, Clayton HB, DeGue S, et al. Interpersonal violence victimization among high school students - youth risk behavior survey, United States, 2019. *MMWR Suppl.* 2020;69(1):28-37.

3. US teen demographics. Act for Youth. 2022. Accessed July 18, 2022. https://actforyouth.net/adolescence/demographics/

4. Preventing intimate partner violence. Centers for Disease Control and Prevention. Updated October 9, 2020. Accessed October 8, 2021. https://www.cdc.gov/violenceprevention/intimatepartnerviolence/fastfact.html

5. Final recommendation statement on intimate partner violence, elder abuse, and abuse of vulnerable adults: screening. US Preventive Services Task Force. October 23, 2018. Accessed September 25, 2021. https://www.uspreventive services-taskforce.org/uspstf/recommendation/intimate-partner-violence-and-abuse-of-elderly-and-vulnerable-adults-screening

6. Campbell JC, Webster D, Koziol-McClain J, et al. Risk factors for femicide in abusive relationships: results from a multisite case control study. *Am J Public Health.* 2003;93(7):1089-1097. doi:10.2105/ajph.93.7.1089

7. Clark CJ, Renner LM, Logeais ME. Intimate partner violence screening and referral practices in an outpatient care setting. *J Interpers Violence.* 2020;35(23-24):5877-5888.

8. Correa NP. Details matter: a quality improvement study on screening for intimate partner violence at a labor and delivery hospital. *J Appl Res Child.* 2020; 11(1):1-11.

9. Substance Abuse and Mental Health Service Administration's concept of trauma and guidance for a trauma-informed approach. SAMHSA. July 2014. Accessed October 8, 2021. https://ncsacw.samhsa.gov/userfiles/files/SAMHSA_Trauma.pdf

10. Six guiding principles of a trauma-informed approach. Centers for Disease Control and Prevention. Updated September 17, 2020. Accessed October 8, 2021. https://www.cdc.gov/cpr/infographics/6_principles_trauma_info.htm

Chapter 8

The Economical and Societal Impacts

Amy Taylor Signore, DNP, MSN, BS, RN, SANE-A, SANE-P

Objectives

After reviewing this chapter, the reader will be able to:

1. *Understand the impacts of interpersonal violence beyond the victim and their family.*
2. *Identify the economic factors that are affected by interpersonal violence.*
3. *Identify the societal ramifications of interpersonal violence.*

Introduction

When domestic violence is discussed, typically physical altercations between a husband and wife come to mind. However, domestic violence can take many forms, such as between same-sex partners, aggression from females towards males, and violence perpetrated by an adult on a child. While the term intimate partner violence is also frequently used in the literature, the term interpersonal violence will be used in this chapter moving forward, in place of both domestic violence and intimate partner violence, to account for the range in which violence can occur. Regardless of who the perpetrator and victim are, the impact of interpersonal violence goes far beyond the household in which it occurs. Interpersonal violence is a global problem that does not discriminate against any age, race, gender, ethnicity, religion, sexual orientation, or socioeconomic status. Whether interpersonal violence takes the form of physical, emotional, sexual, or financial abuse, it can have extensive ramifications that are felt throughout society and the economy. Interpersonal violence comes with a tremendous cost that is extremely difficult to gauge accurately.

Economic Impact

Although victims of interpersonal violence will bear the initial financial impact of their trauma, there is a ripple effect throughout the economy with each victim. It is estimated that interpersonal violence costs in the United States total $3.6 trillion over victims' lifetimes, which can be seen in greater detail in **Figure 8-1**. These costs affect women disproportionately, with women incurring an average of $103 767 and men incurring an average of $23 414 over their lifetimes. Of the $3.6 trillion, government resources pay approximately 37% of the lifetime economic burden.[1]

There are many factors to consider when addressing the costs associated with interpersonal violence, which are incurred across the lifespan of victims.[2] Costs can be categorized as direct, indirect, or opportunity. ***Direct costs*** are tangible and incurred when a victim utilizes services to treat or protect themselves after an incident of violence. Incidents involving injuries are high, with 75% of females and 48% of males experiencing injuries that could require them to seek medical treatment.[3] These medical costs total 59% of the lifetime economic burden on victims and are estimated at $2.1 trillion.[1] While the victim bears the responsibility of paying for using these services, these bills are often paid for with public funding or absorbed through uncompensated care financing, resulting in higher fees for medical services for the public.

Another factor influencing costs is that many cases require the engagement of social services to provide temporary housing placement, parental counseling, legal advocacy, or child protection. Other direct costs are incurred within the judicial system through law enforcement, the issuing of orders of protection, sentencing of perpetrators, and perpetrator incarcerations. Criminal justice activities account for only 2%, or $73 billion, of the lifetime economic burden of interpersonal violence in the United States.[1]

Figure 8-1. *The Lifetime Economic Burden of Intimate Partner Violence.*[1]

The Lifetime Economic Burden of Intimate Partner Violence

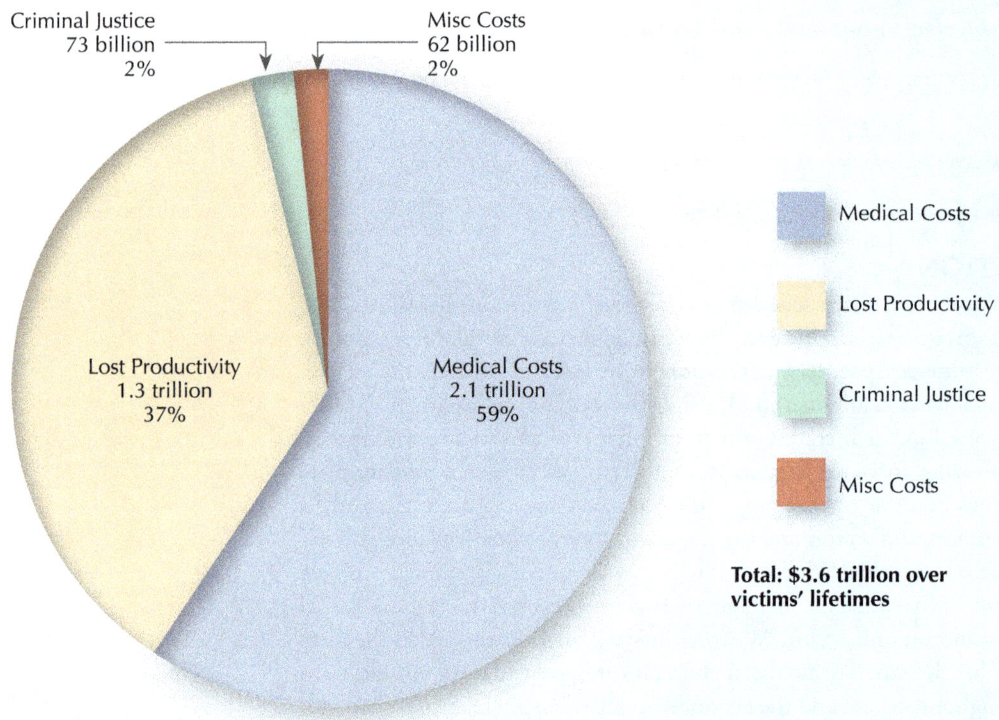

Total: $3.6 trillion over victims' lifetimes

Figure 8-1

While the government absorbs the majority of direct costs, victims often feel the brunt of the indirect costs.[2] Some of these ***indirect costs*** are quantifiable, such as damages to household items, settlement of outstanding debts, moving fees, and lost wages. The Victims of Crime Act provides states with funding to help compensate victims for these out-of-pocket costs.[4] However, most of these programs require victims to report the crime within a predetermined time. Because reporting can be problematic for victims of interpersonal violence, with approximately 50% of incidents going unreported out of fear, coercion, threats, or lack of resources, many victims do not access this funding.[5] Intangible costs can be even more difficult to quantify. Victims often experience the lifelong consequences of chronic pain, anxiety, depression, addiction, suicide attempts, and low self-esteem, which require continued medical and psychological services.

Opportunity costs come into play when victims find themselves at a disadvantage due to experiencing interpersonal violence.[2] For example, victims may be unable to pursue higher education, limiting future earning opportunities, or they may miss out

Figure 8-2. *Signore, Amy. "Financial Despair"*

on promotions at work or experience a job loss due to decreased productivity or lost time. A decrease in a victim's productivity can take several forms: absenteeism, sleep deprivation, concerns about child care, embarrassment, and tardiness. It is estimated that victims of interpersonal violence lose a total of 8 million days of work annually.[6] This loss of productivity can have a domino effect in the corporate sector. Missed work disrupts the supply chain. A decrease in distribution and production leads to late deliveries, which negatively impacts customer satisfaction and leads to a loss of business.[2] Of the $3.6 trillion lifetime economic burden of interpersonal violence, $1.3 trillion is attributable to a loss of productivity among victims and perpetrators.[1]

A decrease in productivity is not the only impact on opportunity costs. Interpersonal violence also increases the number of claims filed through insurance, which leads to higher employee benefit costs and insurance premiums. Often, victims remain employed with the same business, leading to the abuser targeting their victim while they are in the workplace. The Corporate Alliance to End Partner Violence conducted a survey[6] on interpersonal violence in the workplace, and 40% of the participants reported experiencing harassment by their abusers while at work. Although rare, this harassment can escalate and lead to attempting homicide in the workplace, endangering both the victim and other bystander employees. Therefore, the threat of interpersonal violence spilling over to the workplace is a cause of concern for corporations, leading to an increase in security costs in an attempt to provide adequate protection for all employees.

Businesses may also choose to provide employees with enhanced training on recognizing and responding to workplace violence. Over time, these added securities and trainings can be very costly to corporations.

Although the total financial cost of interpersonal violence can only be estimated, its detrimental impact on the economy is significant. Whether it is the individual paying medical bills and replacing damaged goods, taxpayers covering the costs of social and judicial services, or corporations experiencing losses in productivity, interpersonal violence is a massive financial issue in the United States.

Societal Impact

Interpersonal violence does not occur in a vacuum. Even though it may begin in a home between 2 people, interpersonal violence slowly will begin to affect other

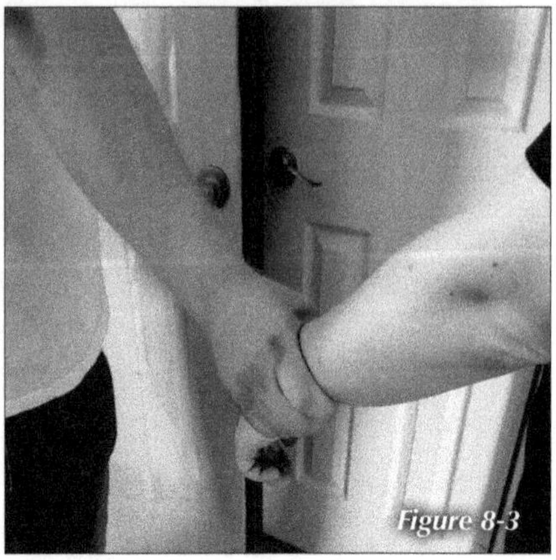

Figure 8-3. *Signore, Amy. "Domineering"*

family members and friends. On a larger scale, it impacts society through increased homelessness, addictions, chronic illnesses, sexually transmitted infections (STIs), disrupted family units, developmental delays and antisocial behavior in children, and potential years of life lost.

Interpersonal violence is one of the primary causes of homelessness for women and children.[7] Statistics from the National Network to End Domestic Violence show that between 22% and 57% of women and children will end up homeless due to interpersonal violence. Often, this is not a one-time occurrence; instead, a victim may return to their abuser only to leave and repeat the homelessness cycle once again.

Victims may first seek safe housing through emergency shelters, which are short-term options which offer victims housing with supportive services like counseling, job training, life skills, education, and childcare.[7] Transitional housing, however, is only a temporary solution to a long-term problem.

Transitional housing has a set time limit, and the victim may require more time to become stable enough to survive on their own. Unfortunately, these services are limited, and more than 1/2 of interpersonal violence victims will not receive resources from any shelters.[8] The victim is then confronted with the choice to return to the abuser or to homelessness.

The stress of experiencing interpersonal violence can adversely affect the health of the victim. Victims may develop unhealthy coping strategies to avoid the negative feelings of low self-esteem that interpersonal violence often creates, such as misuse of substances as a means of escape or to numb the pain that a victim is feeling.[9] While these coping skills may provide the victim with some immediate relief, the misuse of substances only opens the victim up to more complex problems. Substance use can leave the victim more vulnerable to sexual exploitation and further victimization. Furthermore, a victim may experience an increase in isolation as family support systems dissipate due to the victim's substance use. These unhealthy coping mechanisms can also jeopardize the victim's parental rights as they then may be unable to properly care for their children. Additionally, addiction puts the victim's health at risk, requiring them to utilize more health care services. Continued addictive behaviors may also lead to job loss. Without a source of income and with limited resources being utilized to support their addiction, victims may turn to criminal activities to pay their bills and support their addiction. Overall, addiction—a common coping mechanism for interpersonal violence—negatively impacts society as it increases child abuse, neglect, and custodial losses, increases the rates of homelessness and poverty, adds strains on coworkers and loss of revenue for businesses, leads to more violent crimes and incarcerations, and creates a significant burden on the health care system.[9]

Impact of Interpersonal Violence on Public Health

Interpersonal violence creates a serious public health issue with victims experiencing physical and psychological injuries related to the sexual or physical violence.[10] Furthermore, the stress from exposure to interpersonal violence can place victims at risk for chronic illnesses like hypertension, cardiac disease, chronic pain, gastrointestinal disorders, and cancer.[9] In particular, reproductive health can be disproportionately affected. Interpersonal violence is linked to increases in adolescent and unintended pregnancies due to forced sexual encounters. Victims have higher rates of miscarriages, intrauterine hemorrhages, stillbirths, and low-weight births.[6] Forced or coerced sex, especially when the victim is not permitted to use protection or to prevent exposure to infections, puts them at further risk for STIs such as HIV.[11] Following exposure, treatment may be withheld from victims, increasing the risk of spreading STIs to the community at large. In addition, interpersonal violence also takes a toll on the mental health of the victim. Victims may experience depression, anxiety, suicidal ideation, and post-traumatic stress disorder.[10] The need for psychological care creates a serious issue for the already over-burdened mental health community.

Interpersonal violence also can have devastating effects on the dynamics of the family. Living under the threat of violence and in an environment of fear and distrust can ultimately destroy the family unit.[12] Furthermore, interpersonal violence poses a significant threat to the safety of a child through purposeful or accidental injury. Even if a child does not directly experience any physical or emotional abuse, the exposure to interpersonal violence comes at a great cost to the child as they may experience anxiety, increased fear, depression, nightmares, regressive behaviors, aggression, anger, appetite changes, isolation, and increased fighting behaviors.[13] Adolescents who are exposed to interpersonal violence may have a decline in grades, a loss of interest in activities, social withdrawal, rebellious behavior, tardiness, and absenteeism.[13] Worse yet, children who witness violence in the home are at a greater risk of abusing or being abused in future relationships.[13] This cycle of abuse can be difficult to break. The stress of interpersonal violence also places affected children at higher risk for poor mental health conditions, diabetes, obesity, heart disease, and other issues requiring the use of health care services. Besides chronic health problems, the exposure to interpersonal violence also has a negative impact on the child's future development, leading to poor performances in school, increases in addiction rates, sexual disorders and integration, and adjustment problems. Children who have been physically abused are at an increased risk of arrest in the future (59% as adolescents and 28% as adults).[14] The devastation created by interpersonal violence is often intergenerational and has long-term societal consequences.

Perhaps the most overwhelming impact of interpersonal violence is the potential years of life lost. While not all incidents of interpersonal violence lead to fatalities, there are a fair number that do and this is costly. A study[15] of 16 states from 2006 to 2015 revealed that 290 000 potential years of life were lost due to interpersonal violence in the United States. This loss was attributed to interpersonal violence victims themselves and associated victims such as children, family members, friends, law enforcement officers, and strangers. In addition to the tragedy of these premature deaths, they also rob society of potential work productivity, family growth, and community development.

Summary

While at times it is difficult to quantify the impact that interpersonal violence has on the economy and society, it is undeniable that its consequences are far-reaching. Interpersonal violence's effects reach throughout the lifespan of victims and their families. The broader economy is strained by limited services and loss of productivity, and society itself bears the burden of homelessness, addiction, and poor physical and mental health outcomes. Interpersonal violence creates a vicious cycle of violence that is extremely difficult to break and can often be repeated through a family's generations.

References

1. Peterson C, Kearns MC, McIntosh WLKW, et al. Lifetime economic burden of intimate partner violence among US adults. *Am J Prev Med.* 2018;55(4):433-444. doi:10.1016/j.amepre.2018.04.049

2. López-Sánchez MJ, Belso-Martínez JA, Hervás-Oliver JL. A review of economic consequences and costs of male violence against women. *Indian J Gender Stud.* 2019;26(3):424-434. doi:10.1177/0971521519861194

3. Preventing intimate partner violence: violence prevention injury. Centers for Disease Control and Prevention. October 9, 2020. Accessed October 3, 2021. https://www.cdc.gov/violenceprevention/intimatepartnerviolence/fastfact.html

4. Victims of Crime Act. Office for Victims of Crime. Accessed September 1, 2023. https://ovc.ojp.gov/program/victims-crime-act-voca-administrators/welcome

5. Truman JL, Morgan RE. Nonfatal domestic violence, 2003-2012. United States Department of Justice Bureau of Statistics. 2014. Accessed September 1, 2023. https://bjs.ojp.gov/content/pub/pdf/ndv0312.pdf

6. Statistics. National Coalition Against Domestic Violence. Accessed October 15, 2021. https://ncadv.org/STATISTICS

7. Homelessness resources: housing and shelter. Substance Abuse and Mental Health Services Administration. Accessed October 27, 2021. https://www.samhsa.gov/homelessness-programs-resources/hpr-resources/housing-shelter

8. Rogers Cof LL. Transitional housing programs and empowering survivors of domestic violence. The United States Department of Justice. 2021. Accessed October 29, 2021. https://www.justice.gov/archives/ovw/blog/transitional-housing-programs-and-empoweri ng-survivors-domestic-violence

9. Araujo Bastos Teixeira CABT, Lasiuk G, Barton S, Neyrian de Fatima Fernandes M, da Silva Gherardi-Donato EC. An exploration of addiction in adults experiencing early-life stress: a metasynthesis. *Rev Lat Am Enfermagem.* 2017;25:e2939. doi:10.1590/1518-8345.2026.2939

10. Effects of violence against women. Office on Women's Health. Accessed December 3, 2021. https://www.womenshealth.gov/relationships-and-safety/effects-violence-against-women

11. Cavanaugh C, Ward K. HIV/STI prevention interventions for women who have experienced intimate partner violence: a systematic review and look at whether the interventions were designed for disseminations. *AIDS Behav.* 2021;25(11): 3605-3616. doi:10.1007/s10461-021-03318-5

12. The effects of domestic and family violence. Family and Community Services. 2019. Accessed October 3, 2021. https://dcj.nsw.gov.au/children-and-families/family-domestic-and-sexual-violence/about-domestic-and-family-violence/the-effects-of-domestic-and-family-violence.html

13. Effects of domestic violence on children. Office on Women's Health. 2019. Accessed October 3, 2021. https://www.womenshealth.gov/relationships-and-safety/domestic-violence/effects-domestic-violence-children

14. Filip O, Popp L, Andrioni F. The domestic violence effects on the development of future adults. *Rev Universitara Sociologie.* 2020;2:306-312.

15. Graham LM, Ranapurwala SI, Zimmer C, et al. Disparities in potential years of life lost due to intimate partner violence: data from 16 states for 2006-2015. *PLoS One.* 2021;16(2):1-13. doi:10.1371/journal.pone.0246477

Chapter 9

Stalking and Interpersonal Violence

Catherine Mortiere, PhD
Richard Sochor

Objectives

After reviewing this chapter, the reader will be able to:

1. *Define and identify examples of stalking and interpersonal violence.*
2. *Identify the importance of stalking typology.*
3. *Identify the various types of relationships between victims and perpetrators that end in stalking behavior.*
4. *Outline the various types of cyberstalking.*

Introduction

Domestic violence (ie, interpersonal violence) is any abusive, violent, coercive, forceful, or threatening act or word inflicted by one member of a family or household on another.[1] It includes physical, emotional, economic, spiritual, and/or sexual abuse. Some examples of this abusive behavior include:

— Constant criticism

— Acting jealous, domineering, or possessive

— Monitoring where their partner goes, who they call, and with whom they spend time

— Imprisoning their partner in their home or keeping them from leaving

— Intimidating their partner to force obedience

— Threatening to hurt their partner, the children, other family members, or pets

— Damaging property when angry

— Forcing or manipulating the victim in a sexual manner

— Not allowing certain religious practices

— Controlling the family income or stealing money from their partner

— Physically abusing others in the home or threatening abuse

— Murder

There are times when interpersonal violence involves stalking another person in the household. Stalking includes the "willful, malicious, and repeated following and harassing of another person that threatens his or her safety."[2] Another definition, presented by Pathé & Mullen,[3] says that stalking is "a constellation of behaviors in which one individual inflicts on another repeated unwanted intrusions and communications." However, stalking is ultimately defined, as most experts and statutes typically emphasize, as a course of conduct involving repeated actions, which must occur on more than 1 occasion.[4] Some examples of stalking behaviors include[5]:

— Following victims

— Loitering near victims' homes and workplaces

— Giving gifts

— Sending letters

— Transmitting emails

— Making phone calls or sending text messages

— Vandalizing property (eg, car or home)

— Watching or following victims from a distance; spying on victims with a listening device, camera, global positioning system (GPS), or smart phone

— Photographing victims or their families

— Making threats

— Approaching or confronting victims in public places, near the victims' homes, or at the victims' workplaces

— Sneaking into the victims' home or car and doing something to scare the victim or let them know the perpetrator was there

— Physical and/or sexual assault

There is a real and significant connection between stalking and interpersonal violence. In fact, intimate partner stalking is the largest category of all stalking cases.[6-8] Stalking often co-occurs with interpersonal violence and can be an indicator of other forms of violence. Many abusers use stalking to intimidate and control their victims. There are many similarities between domestic violence and stalking. Domestic violence refers to abusive conduct toward a person with whom the perpetrator has either resided or has had an intimate relationship, whereas stalking behavior can occur in all circumstances, including with a stranger or acquaintance. Although there are differences between domestic violence and stalking, such as the victim's relationship to the perpetrator, this chapter will focus on and refer to the overlapping stalking behaviors.

Stalking

Although the meaning of the word stalking has expanded, there is no reason to believe that stalking (by modern definition) is an entirely recent phenomenon.[9] This pattern of behavior likely goes back as far as all of human history. One of the first accounts of what would be known today as a "celebrity stalker" is described in the book *Queen Victoria's Stalker: The Strange Case of the Boy Jones*,[10] which depicts events following the 1838 coronation of Queen Victoria and the difficulties that she confronted with a young stalker. The stalker, "Boy Jones," managed to sneak into Buckingham Palace on a number of occasions. On 2 of these instances, he was found hiding in the Queen's dressing room, attempting to steal her underwear. Due to the fact that "simple trespass" was not yet a criminal offense, he continued to be a problem until he was kidnapped by government men and forced to serve as a sailor in the Royal Navy.

It is difficult to gauge the prevalence of stalking behavior throughout history, especially when today's perpetual media coverage of stories such as these would have many believe that this behavior is more common than ever. Some consider that this may stand as a reflection of changes in our modern society. One well-known case was of the young actress Rebecca Schaeffer, who in 1989 was murdered at her door by Robert Bardo, who had stalked her for 3 years prior. Robert Bardo was a diagnosed schizophrenic (paranoid type) young man who "fell in love" with Schaeffer after seeing her on television. However, Bardo's adoration turned to anger when he saw a movie in which Schaeffer acted in a bedroom scene. This ruined his perception of Schaeffer as the perfect woman. He became convinced that she had become another "Hollywood tramp" and that she had to be punished. Bardo hired a private detective, who got the actress's address from California's motor vehicle records. He then went to Schaeffer's apartment, rang the bell, and fatally shot her when she came to the door.[11]

Nonuniformity and variability in the fundamental definition of stalking as a criminal offense has the potential to create problems and confusion. What one state considers stalking (ie, wrongful) behavior may be legally acceptable in others. Consistency in legislation helps build confidence in the general public and potential victims who feel they need to protect themselves. Perpetrators often know the particulars of the law better than some of the officers sworn to enforce it. This is akin to the strategy of some pedophiles who are keenly aware of the age-of-consent laws in various states. Consequently, stalkers are commonly aware of in what states they can get away with certain behavior without being arrested or what laws the local police may enforce more than others.

Many behaviors that constitute stalking are not necessarily illegal, and in many instances, they would be quite normal or welcome in a contemporary social context. A friend or partner that shows up unexpectedly or leaves a gift would not necessarily evoke fear in the same way that a stalker doing the same would. These gestures from a friend or partner are generally considered a kind or caring gesture, but with a stalker, the intended message of such a gesture can be more ominous (eg, "I know where you are."). Careful examination of seemingly caring gestures is needed to determine the motivation of a stalker's behavior. Unfortunately, the threatening subtext of such messages is often lost when divorced from the context of repeated, unwanted intrusions. From a legal perspective, this claim is often difficult to support.

Fox et al[12] draw attention to the way in which the inconsistencies with defining stalking have led researchers to measure the phenomenon using a variety of different methods. They posit the argument that although "measuring stalking with a variety of methods facilitates a deeper understanding of the crime, methodological inconsistencies within each of these various measurement methods have largely omitted discussions about the validity and reliability of measurement and the generalizability of published results."[12] Hence, unifying data on stalking is certainly an essential, yet complicated, endeavor for the field of research and legislation to surmount. A consensus on defining stalking would further improve the way in which this problem is approached by all branches of government.

Statistics

Given the fact that definitions of stalking often vary widely, so too do estimates regarding the prevalence of stalking behavior. Prior large-scale representative international studies of stalking behavior indicated that between 2% to 13% of males and 8% to 32% of females will be victimized by a stalker at some point in their adult lives.[13-21]

Recent reports such as the National Intimate Partner and Sexual Violence Survey have presented data on the national prevalence of intimate partner violence, sexual violence, and stalking among women and men in the United States. An estimated 6 to 7.5 million people are stalked per year in the United States.[5,22-27]

Although much is being learned regarding stalking behavior and its prevalence, the body of research is still relatively young and often inconsistent, in part, due to the difficulties involved in properly defining stalking. Unlike other crimes such as physical assault, the perception and emotional reaction to stalking are extremely subjective.

Table 9-1. Stalking Statistics[5,22-27]

Victim Statistics	— Nearly 1 in 6 women and 1 in 17 men have experienced stalking victimization in their life — 50% were stalked before age 25 — About 1 in 4 women and 1 in 10 men experienced contact sexual violence, physical violence, and/or stalking by an intimate partner and reported an intimate partner violence-related impact during their lifetime — 1 in 3 women experienced contact sexual violence, physical violence, and/or stalking by an intimate partner during their lifetime — 1 in 5 women experienced completed or attempted rape — 1 in 6 women were stalked — 1 in 17 men were stalked — 1 in 14 men were made to sexually penetrate someone else — 67% of victims of both traditional stalking and stalking with technology were fearful of being killed or physically harmed — 31% of stalked women were also sexually assaulted — 47% are stalked during a relationship — 46% of victims experienced 1 or more violent incidents by their stalker — 67% of intimate partner femicide victims were stalked by their partner — 54% of femicide victims reported being stalked before being murdered by their stalker — 57% of offenders are current or former intimate partners of the victim

Stalking Typologies

Stalking encompasses a wide range of assorted behaviors, ranging from the seemingly mundane to the violent and potentially fatal. When studying a complex phenomenon such as stalking, it is important to distinguish between its different varieties. This is important not only for the purposes of describing and explaining the phenomena, but also to determine the level of danger when doing a risk assessment.

The way in which stalkers are classified often varies according to the particular needs and concerns of the group utilizing the classification system. For example, law enforcement officers, mental health professionals, and victim advocates all have differing concerns regarding stalkers. These fields have each developed and embraced different classifications that address specific issues and concerns for their area of expertise, all while preserving the technical terminology that is often specific within a particular domain.[4]

With the lack of any complete explanatory theory of stalking, a large number of typologies have been offered. In their 2007 review, Spitzburg & Cupach[12] identified over 20 different stalker typologies. The majority of these different typologies can fit into 3 general categories: "those that classify according to an underlying mental disorder; those that classify according to the stalker's prior relationship with the victim; and those that classify according to the primary motivation for stalking."[4]

These categories are useful in contextualizing stalking behavior in order to gain a better understanding of a stalker's motivation.

Underlying Mental Disorder

Many stalkers do not fit exclusively into 1 diagnostic category. Cases are best understood when taking into account the nature of the subject's preoccupation and prior relationship with their victim. It is believed that, "It is the relationship between the 2 parties, real or imagined, that best informs our understanding of stalkers and their motivations. From this frame of reference, the various stalker/victim types were developed."[28]

Table 9-2. Types of Mental Disorders in Stalking[28]

Type	Description	Victims	Other Factors
Simple Obsessional	Victim and perpetrator have some prior knowledge of one another	Significant partners, casual acquaintances, business associates, professional contacts, friends, neighbors	Most common Often most dangerous Perpetrator becomes angered as a result of a loss of control, an attack on their self-image, or a sense of mistreatment
Love Obsessional	No existing relationship between perpetrator and victim	Celebrities or other public figures known to the stalker through the radio, movies, or television	Many suffer from schizophrenia, a psychotic disorder, or bipolar disorder, which can have psychotic features
Erotomaniac	Perpetrator holds the delusional belief that they are in love with the victim and the victim loves them in return	Public figures and celebrities are often (though not exclusively) the victims	No prior relationship with the victim Stalkers meet DSM-III-R criteria for Delusional (Paranoid) Disorder, Erotomaniac Type

Primary Motivation for Stalking

Mullen et al[4,29] offer their own version of a stalker typology, which adds the dimension of motivation of pursuit. Their categorizations were developed from their experiences with stalkers in a clinical setting. Most of the stalkers were referred through the courts, as the clinic had a known interest in stalkers.[30] The clinic also provided services to stalking victims. They argue that this classification system is capable of serving both forensic and mental health purposes.

The primary types of stalkers proposed by these authors were: the rejected, the resentful, the intimacy seeker, the incompetent suitor, and the predator. These categories attempt to take into account the primary motivation behind the behavior of the stalker, which the authors identified as the first of 3 axes (**Table 9-3**).[4] They posited that the context in which the stalking arises is also of relevance. This context helps to explain the stalker's ultimate goals and the manner in which these goals may be achieved. The authors emphasized that this information is relevant whether or not the perpetrator's judgment is distorted or even delusional.

These differing typologies have their own strengths and weaknesses, and some may prove more useful depending on the circumstances and available information. Although they offer no unifying theory on stalking, typologies can provide a general guide to the expected course and duration of harassment, help determine the probability of violence, and might ultimately provide insight into the most appropriate intervention strategies and treatments for a given stalker type.[31]

Table 9-3. Stalker Typologies[4,29]

AXIS I: PRIMARY TYPES OF STALKERS:
The Rejected: Responding to an unwelcome end to a close relationship by attempting to reconcile the relationship or exacting revenge for a perceived rejection
The Resentful: Responding to a perceived insult or injury by actions aimed not just at revenge, but at vindication
The Intimacy Seeker: Responding to loneliness by attempting to establish a close relationship
The Incompetent Suitor: Would-be suitors seeking a partner by methods that are likely to be counterproductive at best and terrifying for their target at worst
The Predatory: Pursuing their desires for both sexual gratification and control
AXIS II: THE STALKER'S RELATIONSHIP TO THE VICTIM:
Prior intimate partners
Professional contacts
Work-related contacts
Casual acquaintances and friends
The famous
Strangers; no contact prior to the onset of the stalking
AXIS III: THE PSYCHIATRIC CONDITION OF THE STALKER:
Psychotic, which includes schizophrenia, delusional disorders, affective psychosis, and organic psychosis
Non-psychotic, being predominantly personality disorders; may also contain both depressive and anxiety disorders, though they are less common

Stalking Risk Assessment

In determining a stalker's level of risk, it is important to examine both static factors (eg, age, sex, race, history of arrests, psychiatric history) and dynamic factors (eg, current mental status, motivation, relationship status, support systems). Static factors may tell an evaluator if a stalker fits into a particular category of risk based on statistical probabilities, but dynamic factors give other information necessary for an entire picture. It is also important to know if a stalker has a current obsession with someone and what course that has taken over time (eg, escalation or de-escalation). If there are unreasonable expectations of a potential victim of stalking, an evaluator should explore the quality of those expectations. It is also important to know if a stalker is offended by the victim's behavior in some way.

Technology and Cyberstalking

With the rapid and continuous advancement in modern technology, stalkers have access to an arsenal of tools with which to pursue, harass, control, violate, and invoke fear in their victims. Unfortunately, it seems that legislation, as well as the empirical research regarding stalking, have been unable to maintain an equal pace with contemporary innovations, leaving many at risk. Computers, the internet, and other technology, such as cell phones, have forever altered the scope, context, and way in which personal information is managed; in many ways, this technology has also made individuals more vulnerable. No matter how carefully information is managed, there are still ways in which new technology can be exploited for purposes of stalking and victimizing. There is an absence of widely accepted criteria for cyberstalking, which means that it is operationalized in various ways, therefore reducing the comparability and generalizability of findings in the quantitative literature.[32]

Cyberstalking

Cyberstalking can be defined as a pattern of threatening behavior or unwanted advances directed at another using email and other forms of electronic communication. The use of electronic devices may, in fact, be the easiest method of stalking. Electronic devices include smart phones, smart devices, air tags and tracking devices, remote monitoring devices, and computer cameras. Many monitoring devices can be obtained easily and legally from online merchants. Technology has advanced over the last few decades. The growth in technology has led to hundreds of next generation media and communication platforms (eg, Facebook, Instagram, Snapchat). There were over 4 billion users of the internet and 3.4 billion active users of social media in 2019. The internet is composed of technology-supported interactions between individuals, many times without the knowledge of all parties.[33]

The use of electronic monitoring or software tools is the cyberstalker's platform to control, manipulate, and coerce the victim. It is a form of harassment, forcing victims to continuously stay in touch or to be observed without consent. There are also hacking programs which make false impersonation easy and able to be done by both strangers and persons who have had casual contact with the victim.[34]

In one study, Sheridan & Grant[35] examined the difference between cyberstalking and other forms of stalking in order to understand if they should be regarded as distinctive phenomena, or if cyberstalking was just another tool in the stalker's arsenal. They concluded that cyberstalking and offline stalking were more similar than different, and cyberstalking is essentially 1 more invasive technique available to stalkers. Some typical examples of cyberstalking techniques include[35]:

— Seeking and compiling information on the victim in order to harass, threaten, and intimidate them online or offline

— Sending repeated unsolicited emails and instant messages

— Electronically sabotaging, such as spamming and sending viruses to the target

— Committing identity theft

— Subscribing the victim to services

— Purchasing goods and services in the victim's name

— Impersonating another online

— Sending or posting hostile material, misinformation, and false messages on social media

— Tricking other internet users into harassing or threatening a victim (eg, by posting the victim's personal details online along with a controversial invitation)

Cyberstalkers can use the internet to instantly, inexpensively, and efficiently harass their victims in a larger, more public forum than other conventional forms of offline stalking. For example, rather than making individual phone calls, an offender can repeatedly send thousands of harassing email messages through scheduled automated programs, sometimes called email bombing, or create false profiles and identities to post on or stalk their victims through social media. Cyberstalkers have the ability to act while being physically far removed from their victims. This makes escaping the reach of the perpetrator a nearly impossible task, but also adds a terrifying element of uncertainty to the victim, who never can be sure of the physical location of their offender. This may also present legal issues regarding jurisdiction. Since cyberstalking can take place across state lines, prosecutors often run into difficulty when enforcing state laws. Furthermore, cyberstalkers have the capability of remaining virtually anonymous. This frequently allows otherwise shy or unassertive individuals to overcome their personal inhibitions, removing any hesitation that many perpetrators might encounter when confronting a victim in person. Also unique to cyberstalking is that online offenders can easily impersonate their victims. This is often used to tarnish the victim's reputation and usually to align other individuals against the victim. Finally, cyberstalkers can incite others to harass the victim. This is often referred to as stalking by proxy.[36]

Electronic Monitoring Devices

Some of the techniques that stalkers/cyberstalkers employ allow them to obtain information from afar, while other technologies require the offender to have a close proximity to the victim. Several of these technologies can infiltrate nearly every aspect of a victim's personal life, making them extremely vulnerable. A perpetrator also has the potential to listen in on conversations with devices such as a baby monitor, walkie-talkie, or radio scanner,[37] or via in-home smart devices such as Alexa, Google Home, and Ring. Stalkers will often use prepaid calling cards or cell phones to make their calls difficult to trace. Additionally, perpetrators can easily conceal the number they are calling from or make it appear that they are calling from any number of their choosing (eg, the victim's family member, friend, coworker, or boss). This specific type of stalking behavior is called caller ID spoofing, which can also be achieved with email accounts by disguising the stalker's incoming messages as another of their choosing.

Devices such as Apple AirTags, Tile, and other E-trackers are small, wireless devices intended for tracking the location of belongings such as wallets or keys. However, they can also be attached to a person's car or hidden in their belongings to monitor their movements and reveal their real-time location.[38]

Cell phones, especially smart phones, have created a wealth of new vulnerabilities to potential victims. If an offender is able to gain temporary physical access to a victim's cell phone, they can install an undetectable suite of software which allows the stalker to monitor all aspects of the victim's life (eg, listen in on phone calls; check text messages, emails, contact lists, and call history). Furthermore, the offender may also have the ability to remotely turn on the phone's microphone while the device is not in use in order to listen in on the surrounding sounds, essentially turning it into a room bug. Perhaps most frighteningly, the software can also give information from the phone's GPS in order to give nearly exact coordinates of the victim's physical location at any time. Another way stalkers can easily and cheaply monitor a victim's behavior is by simply placing standalone GPS devices onto a target's car. These devices can secretly be attached to the outside of a vehicle or hidden inside somewhere (eg, in the dashboard, trunk, or under seats). These devices can be quickly installed any time the victim's vehicle is unattended and thereby monitor the location of a target in real time.

Impact of Stalking on the Victim

Much like traditional stalking and harassment offline, there are a number of negative psychological impacts on victims' mental health. Some of the negative effects may include flashbacks, depression, nightmares, anxiety, and worse, suicide. Although this chapter does not focus on the impact of victims, it is worth mentioning the extent of which cyberstalking can frighten and terrorize. The fear that cyberstalking invokes in its victims significantly interferes with victims' level of trust in forging online and offline relationships.

Case Studies

Case Study 9-1

Mary had been employed at a hospital for many years. She suddenly found herself being stalked by a hospital official named Raymond. Mary began hearing from her colleagues that this official was telling people that he had known her for years, even though this was prior to her tenure at the hospital. Mary began seeing Raymond nearly every day in various places around the hospital. Raymond tried numerous times to force Mary to say hello or good morning. She would ignore him, but sometimes he would raise his voice and follow her down the hallway yelling, "What, you don't like me?" or "You can't say good morning?" Mary began to feel increasingly more uncomfortable. She tried changing her routine to make it difficult for him to predict when she walked through various areas, but it only took a couple of days for him to catch on and place himself in her path.

Over time, it escalated to the point where she would walk into work almost every day and find him in her path, many times placing his body in the middle of the hallway forcing her to walk around him. Mary wondered how it was that Raymond would know where she was going to be and when. She later realized that he had access to the security camera system, so he could monitor her path and routine changes. When Mary would speak during staff meetings, Raymond would find ways to insert himself into the conversation and patronize or insult her. The harassment began to get so intense that Mary decided to seek the assistance of her workplace's human resources department (HR). Mary sent emails to HR detailing Raymond's actions but never got a response. As Raymond's behavior continued worsening, Mary decided to make a second report to HR in person. Mary had to walk by Raymond's office to get to HR, and 10 minutes later, Raymond walked into the office where they were meeting and disrupted their conversation.

The following day, Mary wrote another email detailing Raymond's behavior and that she was feeling stalked, which was ignored. One day, Mary found that her vehicle had been urinated on. She believed it was Raymond retaliating since she had reported him. A fellow employee came to Mary and told her some strikingly similar accounts by Raymond toward her. She also told Mary that there was a third person with the same complaints about Raymond. Mary put her complaint in writing to the next organizational level, including the accounts of the other employees. Before too long Raymond disappeared for several weeks. After his return, he mostly stayed in his office, and his stalking behavior become much subtler. Mary was never contacted by HR or anyone else to investigate her claims.

Discussion

Mary was in a difficult situation as her stalker was an official at the hospital where she worked. As is always the case when there is a power differential, it was difficult for Mary to report stalking behavior by someone to whom she would typically report such behavior. Additionally, Raymond had access to the security footage, which would normally be used to prove such incidents, so he likely erased whatever was incriminating. It was difficult to prove that his behavior was stalking because he had placed himself in a professional position to have reason to be in all areas of the building. He would abuse his status and authority to get subordinates to assist him in the intimidation of Mary. Unfortunately for Mary, HR also attended the same supervisory meetings as Raymond, which made it difficult for them to discipline one of their own. Raymond's behavior meets several criteria for stalking, such as tracking Mary's whereabouts, committing a form of vandalism by urinating on her vehicle, approaching and confronting Mary in several areas of the hospital, and loitering in areas where Mary needed to walk through.

Case Study 9-2

Julie was working on her doctorate and had just begun her internship at a hospital. During the internship, the students were placed under the supervision of Lumas, a medical doctor who had an administrative position in the hospital. Julie worked long hours and was involved in research. There were several times that Lumas would appear out of nowhere and walk around in front of Julie's office. He repeatedly asked Julie to go out and have a drink with him; however, Julie told him that she was only interested in completing her internship and not engaging in a relationship with him. He ignored Julie's reply and stated that he was married but still liked to go out and have fun. On one occasion, Lumas ordered Julie to meet him in his office to discuss the research she was working on. Upon concluding a phone call, he rolled his chair over to Julie, grabbed her, put his hands over her clothing and squeezed her breasts, attempted to force a kiss on her with an open mouth, and attempted to touch her vagina through her clothing. While this was happening, there was suddenly a loud knock on his office door that startled him, and he covered Julie's mouth tightly with his hand to keep her quiet, making it difficult for her to breathe. After the footsteps outside his door sounded as if they were leading away, Julie grabbed her bag and ran out of his office.

Julie immediately reported the incident to the Affirmative Action Officer as well as the head of the Internal Review Board (IRB) for her research study. Both of them warned Julie not to make a complaint against Lumas as she was an intern and therefore an "at-will employee." They also told her that Lumas was hand-picked by the Executive Director of the hospital for his position. Julie decided to try and get through the internship and keep quiet about the incident, but a few days later, Julie was at home talking with an attorney when her apartment buzzer rang. She looked down from her 4th floor balcony and saw Lumas with a bouquet of flowers. Julie later learned that he had taken her home address from IRB materials she had submitted to the hospital for research. Her attorney instructed her to let him in and hand him the telephone so that he could speak to Lumas and officially put him on notice that Julie wanted to be left alone. After the call, Lumas immediately left the apartment building sufficiently frightened and did not return.

Julie changed her schedule and avoided seeing Lumas as much as possible. He called her several times offering "help" to get her a job and to assist her with her work, but he did not have another opportunity for physical contact. Julie was told by her fellow intern that Lumas was pursuing her as well, which seemed to take his attention. Later, there would be complaints from others about his inappropriate behavior and physical advances, but he was still allowed to continue working at the hospital until he retired.

Discussion

Julie was subordinate to Lumas as a student in the facility. Lumas had direct authority and control over Julie and her research. The incidents described above include sexual assault and stalking (ie, he followed her, called her, summoned her to his office, attempted to give her unwanted gifts [flowers], and accessed her personal information from hospital records). He abused his position to stalk and intimidate her in several ways. Julie reported the sexual assault to 2 key people in administration; however, she was told to say nothing if she wanted to continue working there as a student. Stalking behavior sometimes continues as a result of the victim's limited resources or lack of support. Reporting Lumas was her only available option, as the power imbalance meant she could not take further action. His predatory behavior continued well after Julie was no longer a student, and he was never held accountable for his actions.

Summary

Stalking is a serious crime facing society today. It serves to isolate and terrorize victims, often for years on end. Stalking is an important area to address as it is often the precursor to a violent outcome. With growing technology, stalking has evolved, and technological advances have made it increasingly more difficult to monitor and thwart unwanted intrusions by stalkers. There is great need for agreement on defining the term and elements of stalking in order to have uniformity within and between states when creating statutes appropriate to deal with this issue. As is key with deterrence for any type of crime, education and awareness are at the forefront.

References

1. Huecker MR, King KC, Jordan GA, Smock W. *Domestic Violence.* StatPearls Publishing; 2022. https://www.ncbi.nlm.nih.gov/books/NBK499891/
2. Meloy JR, Gothard S. A demographic and clinical comparison of obsessional followers and offenders with mental disorders. *Am J Psychiatry.* 1995:152(2):258-263. doi:10.1176/ajp.152.2.258
3. Pathé M, Mullen PE. The impact of stalkers on their victims. *Br J Psychiatry.* 1997;170(1):12-17. doi:10.1192/bjp.170.1.12
4. Mullen PE, Pathé M, Purcell R. *Stalkers and Their Victims.* 2nd ed. Cambridge University Press; 2009.
5. Smith SG, Zhang X, Basile KC, et al. The national intimate partner and sexual violence survey (NISVS): 2015 data brief - updated release. Centers for Disease Control and Prevention. 2018. https://www.cdc.gov/violenceprevention/datasources/nisvs/2015NISVSdatabrief.html
6. Mohandie K, Meloy J, McGowan M, Williams J. The RECON typology of stalking: reliability and validity based upon a large sample of North American stalkers. *J Forensic Sci.* 2006;51(1):147-155. doi:10.1111/j.1556-4029.2005.00030.x

7. Roberts AR, Dziegielewski SR. Changing stalking patterns and prosecutorial decisions: bridging the present to future. *Vict Offenders.* 2006;1(1):47-60.

8. Tjaden P, Thoennes N. Stalking in America: findings from the national violence against women survey. National Institute of Justice. 1998. https://www.ojp.gov/ncjrs/virtual-library/abstracts/stalking-america-findings-national-violence-against-women-survey

9. Meloy JR. Stalking: An old behavior, a new crime. *Psychiatr Clin North Am.* 1999;22(1): 85-99. doi:10.1016/s0193-953x(05)70061-7

10. Bondeson J. *Queen Victoria's Stalker: The Strange Case of the Boy Jones.* Kent State University Press; 2011.

11. Meloy J, Sheridan L, Hoffman J. *Stalking, Threatening, and Attacking Public Figures: A Psychological and Behavioral Analysis.* Oxford University Press; 2008.

12. Fox KA, Nobles MR, Fisher BS. Method behind the madness: an examination of stalking measurements. *Aggress Violent Behav.* 2011;16(1):74-84. doi:10.1016/j.avb.2010.12.004

13. Budd T, Mattinson J. *Stalking: Findings from the 1998 British Crime Survey.* Home Office Research, Research Development and Statistics Directorate: Research Findings No. 129; 2000.

14. Elliott L, Brantley C. *Sex on Campus: The Naked Truth About the Real Sex Lives of College Students.* Random House; 1997.

15. Fisher BS, Cullen FT, Turner MG. The sexual victimization of college women. US Department of Justice. December 2000. https://www.ojp.gov/ncjrs/virtual-library/abstracts/sexual-victimization-college-women

16. Hackett K. Criminal harassment. *Juristat.* 2000;20(11):1-16.

17. Kohn M, Flood H, Chase J, McMahon PM. Prevalence and health consequences of stalking-Louisiana, 1998–1999. *MMWR Morb Mortal Wkly Rep.* 2000;49(29):653-655. https://www.cdc.gov/mmwr/preview/mmwrhtml/mm4929a1.htm

18. Kong R. Criminal harassment. *Juristat.* 1996;16(12):1-13.

19. McLennan W. *Crimes Family Violence Act: 1995/96 Monitoring Report.* Victoria, Australia: Magistrates' and Children's Courts; 1996.

20. McLennan W. *Women's Safety Survey.* Australian Bureau of Statistics; 1996.

21. Purcell R, Pathé M, Mullen PE. The prevalence and nature of stalking in the Australian community. *Aust N Z J Psychiatry.* 2002;36(1):114-120. doi:10.1046/j.1440-1614.2002.00985.x

22. Baum K, Catalano S, Rand M, Rose K. Stalking victimization in the United States. Bureau of Justice Statistics. 2009. https://ovc.ojp.gov/sites/g/files/xyckuh226/files/pubs/helpseries/HelpBrochure_Stalking.html

23. Brewster MP. Power and control dynamics in pre-stalking and stalking situations. *J Fam Violence.* 2003;18(4)207-217. doi:10.1023/A:1024064214054

24. McFarlane J, Campbell JC, Wilt S, et al. Stalking and intimate partner femicide. *Homicide Stud.* 1999;3(4):300-316. doi:10.1177/1088767999003004003

25. Morgan RE, Truman JL. Stalking victimization, 2019. US Department of Justice. 2022. Accessed July 1, 2022. https://bjs.ojp.gov/content/pub/pdf/sv19.pdf

26. Stalking and intimate parter violence: Fact sheet - stalking awareness. Stalking Prevention Awareness and Resource Center. 2017. Accessed July 1, 2022.

https://www.stalkingawareness.org/wp-content/uploads/2018/11/Stalking-IPV-Fact-Sheet.pdf

27. Domestic violence. National Coalition Against Domestic Violence. 2020. Accessed July 1, 2022. https://assets.speakcdn.com/assets/2497/domestic_violence-2020080709350855.pdf?1596811079991

28. Zona MA, Palarea RE, Lane JC. Psychiatric diagnosis and the offender-victim typology of stalking. In: Meloy JR, ed. *The Psychology of Stalking: Clinical and Forensic Perspectives.* Academic Press; 1998:69-84.

29. Mullen PE, Pathé M, Purcell R, Stuart GW. Study of stalkers. *Am J Psychiatry.* 1999;156(8):1244-1249. doi:10.1176/ajp.156.8.1244

30. Warren LJ, MacKenzie R, Mullen PE, Ogloff JRP. The problem behavior model: the development of a stalkers clinic and a threateners clinic. *Behav Sci Law.* 2005;23:387-397. doi:10.1002/bsl.593

31. McEwan TE, Pathé M, Ogloff JRP. Advances in stalking risk assessment. *Behav Sci Law.* 2011;29(2):180-201. doi:10.1002/bsl.973

32. Wilson C, Sheridan L, Garratt-Reed D. What is cyberstalking? A review of measurements. *J Interpers Violence.* 2022;37(11-12):NP9763-NP9783. doi:10.1177/0886260520985489

33. Kaur P, Dhir A, Tandon A, Alzeiby EA, Abohassan AA. A systematic literature review on cyberstalking: an analysis of past achievements and future promises. *Technol Forecast Soc Change.* 163:120426. doi:10.1016/j.techfore.2020.120426

34. Silva Santos IL, Pimentel CE, Mariano TE. Cyberstalking scale: development and relations with gender, Fomo and social media engagement. *Current Psychology.* 2023;42(6):4802-4810. doi:10.1007/s12144-021-01823-3

35. Sheridan LP, Grant TD. Is cyberstalking different? *Psychol Crime Law.* 2007;13(6):627-640. doi:10.1080/10683160701340528

36. Goodno NH. Cyberstalking, a new crime: evaluating the effectiveness of current state and federal laws. *Mo Law Rev.* 2006;72(1):125-197.

37. Southworth C, Finn J, Dawson S, Fraser C, Tucker S. Intimate partner violence, technology, and stalking. *Violence Against Women.* 2007;13(8):842-856. doi:10.1177/1077801207302045

38. Hanson EJ, Finklea K. Stalking concerns raised by bluetooth tracking technologies: in brief. Congressional Research Service. July 1, 2022. https://crsreports.congress.gov/

Chapter 10

Dating Violence Among High School and College Students

Tracie L. Nicolai, PhD, EdD

Objectives

After reviewing this chapter, the reader will be able to:

1. *Define dating violence and the types of dating violence.*
2. *Understand the prevalence of dating violence among high school and college students.*
3. *List the ways in which to intervene at school and home.*

Introduction

The term ***dating violence*** is defined as violence committed by a person who is or has been in a social relationship of a romantic or intimate nature with the victim. The existence of such a relationship shall be determined based on the following factors: the length of the relationship; the type of relationship; and the frequency of interaction between the persons involved in the relationship.[1]

Intimate partner violence (IPV) is the most common form of violence against women. It occurs in all settings and among all socioeconomic, religious, and cultural groups. Globally, 6% of women report having been sexually assaulted by someone other than a partner, although data for non-partner sexual violence are more limited. Intimate partner and sexual violence are mostly perpetrated by men against women.[2] Although women can be violent in relationships with men, it is often due to self-defense. In contrast, men are far more likely to experience violent acts by strangers or acquaintances than by someone close to them.[3] IPV does occur in same-sex partnerships as well. The perception toward same-sex IPV indicates that more resources and education is needed. However, same-sex IPV appears to share characteristics with heterosexual IPV.

Types of Dating Violence and Abuse

Abuse is a pattern of behavior used by one person to gain and maintain power and control over another. One domestic violence resource[4] states that there are 6 different types of abuse: physical, sexual, verbal/emotional, mental, financial, and cultural/identity abuse. The perpetrator of abuse may use a combination of male privilege, isolation, coercion/threats, intimidation, economic abuse, emotional abuse, denying/blaming or minimizing, harassment, threats, limitation of independence, or violation of privacy in order to maintain the pattern of control and abuse. Signs of abuse include intensity, manipulation, sabotage, guilting, deflecting responsibility, belittling, volatility, possessiveness, and betrayal. If children are involved in the relationship, the abuser may also use threats against the child(ren)'s safety or the victim's custody as a point of manipulation. The Power and Control Wheel can be used to help identify patterns of behavior or abuse in a relationship.[5]

Physical Abuse

Across the world, between 13% and 61% of women who are in intimate relationships have experienced physical violence at the hands of their partner.[2] Dynamics of the individual woman, family, community, and culture interact with each other to either increase or reduce the risk of violence.

Physical abuse is the intentional use of force with the potential to cause death, disability, injury, or harm.[6] Physical abuse can include[4]:

— Punching/hitting/slapping

— Kicking

— Strangling or physically restraining a partner against their will

— Driving recklessly

— Invading someone's physical space

— Making someone feel physically unsafe in any other way

Physical violence is the form of violence most often associated with the word "abuse." However, physical force is only 1 means of power and control, and it is often not the first form of abuse that the perpetrator will use.[4]

Sexual Abuse

While sexual abuse can be a form of physical abuse due to its physical components, it can also include nonphysical components (eg, noncontact acts of a sexual nature). ***Sexual abuse*** is defined by the Centers for Disease Control and Prevention (CDC)[6] as an act that is committed or attempted by another person without the freely given consent of the victim or an act committed against a victim who is unable to consent or refuse. This type of abuse can involve rape, other forced sexual acts (including those that are alcohol/drug facilitated), and the act of withholding or using sex as a weapon. An abusive partner might also use sex in a way that overlaps with emotional abuse, such as to judge their partner and assign value to them (eg, criticizing their partner by saying they are not good enough at sex, saying that sex is the only thing they are good for).

Because sex is layered with emotional and cultural implications, there are a number of ways the feelings surrounding it can be uniquely used for power and control. For example, it was not until 1993 that marital rape became illegal in all 50 states. Furthermore, some partners in an intimate relationship assume that they are entitled to sex and therefore do not recognize that entitlement as a larger pattern of power and control. According to the World Health Organization (WHO),[2] roughly 30% of women worldwide have experienced sexual violence by an intimate partner at least once in their lifetime. In the United States, more than 1 in 3 women and 1 in 4 men have experienced sexual violence involving physical contact during their lifetimes.[7]

Psychological Abuse

Psychological (ie, mental) abuse occurs when a partner, through a series of actions or words, wears away at the other partner's sense of mental wellbeing and health. Globally, violence against women is disturbingly excessive. Of women aged 15 to 49 years, 27% have been in relationships that have resulted in violence that caused physical, sexual, or psychological harm.[8]

Psychological harm can include acts of aggression, psychological abuse, controlling behaviors and sexual coercion.[2] This type of abuse often uses gaslighting, a sort of manipulation designed to make someone unsure of their own perception, memory, or understanding of events, to make the victim doubt their own sanity. For example, perpetrators may deliberately move personal items (eg, car keys, car, purse), dim the lights, or commit other acts and then deny doing so. The result of this, especially over a sustained period of time and in conjunction with the isolation that abusers tend to enforce, is that the victim begins to not trust their own judgements, leading to an increased dependence on the abuser. Victims also tend to hesitate to communicate the abuse they are experiencing for fear that they will not be believed.

Verbal/Emotional Abuse

Verbal abuse is the use of verbal communication with the intent to harm another person mentally or emotionally while exerting control over them. With this type of abuse, the perpetrator uses words as their weapons. Over time, the victim begins to believe the abuser's lies (eg, that they are worthless, stupid, ugly, or that no one would want them if they left the relationship). The effects of verbal abuse are hard to identify and difficult to prove. Oftentimes, the emotional trauma takes longer to heal than physical marks of abuse.[4,6]

Financial/Economic Abuse

Because abuse thrives on power, an abuser will use any means necessary to maintain control over their victim. This often includes the perpetrator taking control of their victim's finances, typically in one of the following ways[4,6]:

— Managing all household budgets

— Not allowing the victim to have access to their own bank account(s) or spending money

— Opening credit cards and acquiring debt in the victim's name

— Not letting the victim have a job or earn their own money

For these reasons, this type of abuse is often why someone is unable to leave an abusive relationship. Particularly for high school and college-age survivors, economic abuse is not uncommon within their intimate partner relationships, with outcomes affecting mental and physical health, parent-child interactions, and quality of life.[4,6] Many survivors have problems with their credit because of an abuser's past behavior. A bad credit history can affect a survivor's ability to get an apartment, a job, a car loan, and any number of other things that are necessary for self-sufficiency. While there are programs to help survivors resolve these issues, social safety nets such as food stamps, cash assistance, and health insurance can provide a much-needed bridge in the meantime.[4,6]

Cultural/Identity Abuse

Cultural abuse is defined as abusers using aspects of a victim's particular cultural identity to inflict suffering or as a means of control. Examples of this type of abuse are[4,6]:

— Refusing to observe the dietary or dress customs of their partner's faith

— Using racial slurs

— Threatening to "out" someone as LGBTQIA+

— Isolating someone who does not speak the dominant language where they live

Dating Violence Among High School Students

Teen dating violence includes physical, psychological or sexual abuse; harassment; or stalking of any person aged 12 to 18 years in the context of a past or present romantic or consensual relationship.[9] Amongst high school students, 1 in 10 have reported experiencing physical violence from a partner in the last year alone.[10]

A 2014 National Institute of Justice-funded[11] longitudinal study of 1162 students in the Midwest examined the prevalence of several kinds of abuse that middle and high school students experienced and perpetrated in their relationships. The study found that 1/3 of students reported experiencing physical violence in a teen dating relationship. More girls reported perpetrating physical dating violence than boys (34% as opposed to 17%). Verbal emotional abuse was the most common form of dating violence the high school students had experienced; 73% of girls and 66% of boys reported experiencing at least 1 instance of verbal abuse. In addition, 64% of girls and 45% of boys reported perpetrating verbal emotional abuse toward a dating partner. Furthermore, nearly 1 in 4 girls and 1 in 7 boys reported being victims of sexual coercion in a teen dating relationship.[12]

Cyberbullying

Technology is changing the way culture functions in society, allowing opportunities for education, communication, and convenience of interaction. Technology also has negative public safety risks. It places students' emotional wellbeing and safety at risk if not used responsibly. Cyberbullying is a form of bullying that occurs with the usage of technological devices including cell phones, computers, and tablets. According to the CDC, an estimated 15.9% of high school students were electronically bullied in 2021.[13] Cyberbullying incorporates posting or sharing negative, false, or malicious content about someone in an effort to cause hurt, embarrassment, or humiliation. Common places for cyberbullying to occur include:

— Social media (eg, Facebook, Instagram, Snapchat, TikTok)

— Instant messaging

— Text messaging

— Email

— Online forums, chat rooms

— Online gaming

Suicidal Ideation

Notable challenges in adolescent development include dating violence and suicidal ideation (ie, thoughts or plans) and, subsequently, their association with each other.[14] This association was evaluated in a study[14] done on a cohort of students between the grades of 9 and 12. The study contained 556 randomly selected students, of which 1/2 identified as male and 1/2 as female. 47.5% of participants identified themselves as White, 37.8% identified themselves as Black, and 11.2% identified themselves as Latino. The participants also reported dating at least once during the time of the study. Self-reported frequency of suicidal ideation, dating, and physical dating violence perpetration and victimization were assessed each spring. The results of this study indicated the following:

— 1/4 of the sample reported suicidal ideation at least once by the end of grade 12.

— Approximately 1/2 of the students reported physical dating violence.

— Female gender, physical dating perpetration, physical dating victimization, and being in grades 9 through 11 vs 12 were significant predictors of suicidal ideation.

— Race was not a significant predictor among adolescents in this sample.

Dating Violence Among College Students

Physical and sexual victimization are serious problems affecting those attending college. In a national sample[15] of college students, 32% of the women reported experiencing physical dating violence from the age of 14 years through their time in college (the average age of the women in this sample was 21.4 years old).

Women who had been previously victimized are at a higher risk for revictimization, with adolescent victimization being a better predictor of college victimization than childhood victimization.[16]

In 2017, Bowling Green State University[17] researched dating violence during the participants' transition from adolescence to young adulthood. Researchers collected data from approximately 1000 individuals ages 25 to 28 who had previously participated in the Toledo Adolescent Relationship Study when they were in 7th, 9th, or 11th grade. This longitudinal sample measured unwanted sexual pressures and physical abuse within relationships. The study also questioned participants about other indicators of relationship characteristics to better understand patterns and consequences of abuse. 56% of participants in this study reported perpetrating or being a victim of some form of relationship abuse during their lives. Nearly 1 in 5 participants had experienced unwanted sexual pressures within a romantic relationship.[17] The imbalance of power and control has always existed in an abusive relationship. It is not easily identifiable at first. While some relationships are clearly abusive from the onset, others get worse over time.

Warning signs include[18] withdrawing from activities such as spending less time with friends, leaving sports teams, or dropping classes; isolating by telling a partner not to engage in social activities or limiting contact with others; or disclosing that sexual assault has happened before. Other warning signs include any mention of a partner trying to limit their contraceptive options, refusing to use safer sexual practices (eg, using condoms or not wanting them to use birth control); a partner pressuring them to do things that make them uncomfortable; a partner controlling their means of communication (eg, the partner answering their phone or text messages or intruding into private conversations); and lastly, visible signs of physical abuse, such as bruises or black eyes.

Interventions

Parent Response

To help ensure their children's safety, parents need to build trusting relationships and communicate with their children about who they are dating and, in general, who they are socializing with outside of school. If their child says they are going somewhere alone or with friends, parents should check in to verify their location. For example, parents can ask their child to share a photo of their location. Parents can also use mobile applications such as Life360 to check their child's location for themselves. Most importantly, parents should trust their instincts and always monitor their child's welfare.

School Response

In the past 10 years, there has been an increase in dating violence and abuse reporting due to the news coverage and social media. When abuse is suspected or reported, the school documents it and notifies the children's parents, as well as the police and Department of Health and Human Services. This activated, coordinated community response from the school allows for a reduction in IPV, provision of early intervention, and emotional support. Victims also get help in involving the criminal justice system in their cases.[19]

When pictures or videos depicting nudity or of graphic nature are shared in a school, this should be reported immediately to the administrators and the police. Students should not delete the pictures or videos right away, as the police will need them for evidence. The student should not share these files with anyone else besides the adult they initially report to, the administration, and the police.

At K-12 schools, there are social emotional learning curricula available to address topics such as teen violence. For example, the "See Something, Say Something" initiative advises students to report inappropriate behavior via a link on the high school website or in the counselor's office.[20] If a student has been sexually assaulted, they should be referred to local agencies for family services; it is also recommended the student receive follow-up therapy. It is essential the student has a relationship with an adult at the school (eg, a school counselor or psychologist) to check in with throughout the day. Additionally, it is important that suicide prevention programs incorporate dating violence education and prevention/intervention strategies starting early in high school, as victims often suffer from poor mental health after being abused.[20]

Student Response

It is important for victims of dating violence to develop a crisis plan so they can prepare to safely exit their abusive relationship. Ideally, parents and educators will have already discussed with students identifying abuse tactics and methods for putting together safety plans. There are new websites and mobile applications available to help with this process, such as the Anemone app.[21] Questions to consider when creating a crisis plan include:

— Where is the nearest exit?

— Where do you live?

— Who can help?

As part of the safety plan, high school and college-age students are advised that if they plan to go to a party or an unfamiliar location, they should stay with someone they arrived with rather than drive home alone or leave with someone they do not know, especially if they plan to drink alcohol or use drugs.

Case Studies

Case Study 10-1

This high school counselor reported that a 15-year-old female student came into her office and stated she and her 17-year-old boyfriend had a fight involving him telling her she was "stupid if she thought she could break up with him." He had taken her car keys away from her and prevented her from leaving his house. The boyfriend later apologized to her for saying she was stupid and that he did not really mean it, he was just upset when he thought about losing her. He then stated he would kill himself if they broke up. She then told the counselor that during class the boyfriend was texting her asking if she still loved him and if they were okay. He then sent her 6 pictures of them and texted her a total of 23 times within her first 3 classes. The female student was feeling anxious and unable to concentrate in the classroom due to his texting, which led to her seeing the counselor. She told the counselor, "So you see, I can't break up with him because he threatened to hurt himself."

Discussion

The counselor listened to and validated the student's concern, and when the student finished communicating her thoughts and concerns, asked what she would do if this same scenario was happening with one of her friends. The counselor asked if she thought this behavior would be acceptable from her friend's boyfriend. They then discussed what healthy relationships should look like and what to do if anyone expresses the desire to hurt themselves, like her boyfriend did. After the appointment, the counselor followed mandated reporting guidelines regarding the boyfriend's abuse and self-harm and made sure that he was provided with the number to the suicide helpline.

Case Study 10-2

Rudy was a 16-year-old transmasculine junior in high school who used he/they pronouns. They disclosed to their mom that they were in a relationship with Zeke, another nonbinary individual. The pair had been dating for 6 months, when one night Rudy stated they were going to go over to their friend Jewel's house to watch movies, and Zeke told Rudy they had to go together, otherwise Zeke would not bring Rudy to work the next day. Rudy did not have their own vehicle, and their family would not be able to bring them to work. When Rudy pleaded with Zeke to let them go to Jewel's house, Zeke said they could go together and stay for 30 minutes because Zeke does not like Rudy's friends. Rudy decided the two of them could stay home and watch the same movie as their friends and simply text them.

Discussion

This is a small example of more subtle dating violence, and it comes in the form of emotional manipulation. By Zeke saying they would not take Rudy to work if they went to their friend's house without them, they are beginning to isolate Rudy, which can later progress to more aggressive forms of dating violence.

Case Study 10-3

A mother described to her family counselor how her 18-year-old daughter had put her hand out to stop her 20-year-old boyfriend from getting closer to her. He then pushed her up against the wall. A friend saw and reported the incident, saying that this was not the first time he had pushed her. Her parents are aware of at least 2 other incidents that occurred at their home. The mother discussed how the daughter believed the boyfriend's explanation that he was upset and was only trying to have a conversation with her, deflecting responsibility and guilt from the boyfriend, while justifying to her mother that, "He's not a bad person. I also pushed him." She then said that when she tried to talk to her daughter and remind her someone else saw the incident, her daughter said it was not as bad as it seemed. The mother felt her child was unsafe and reported the abuse.

Discussion

Parents can have a large part in the safety planning process, and they need to have a good understanding of trauma bonding and what it can do. Trauma bonding is a general phenomenon of victims developing emotional attachments to their abusers through a cycle of abuse and reconciliation.[22] In this case, the parents did not understand the trauma bond that their daughter had formed and simply had her cut off contact with the boy. Their daughter did not tell her friends about what her parents had said, and she kept seeing her boyfriend. The family counselor reminded her parents that their daughter is an adult and in her first relationship with a man, and so they must be cognizant of what this relationship means to her and how the trauma bond is affecting her.

Summary

An abusive relationship can include any or all types of abusive behavior. Often, violence escalates over time until the perpetrator has complete power and control over their partner. Since dating violence can leave deleterious emotional effects on the victim, researchers should continue to look for factors that can reduce revictimization in high school and college students.[16]

The best thing to do for the victim is to:

— Listen to and believe the victim.

— Be supportive and explain abuse is never acceptable.

— Focus on the victim and connect them with resources.

Statements such as "This is not your fault" and "I am worried things could get worse" can help when speaking to someone who is experiencing dating violence. One should remember that when someone is trying to leave an abusive relationship, it is the most dangerous time for them. A support person should ground them with trauma-informed questions, beginning by asking simple questions they can answer (eg, Are you thirsty? Do you need water?) before moving on to heavier topics. Since it can be difficult for them to give a logical, linear account of the violence they experienced, it can also be helpful to ask questions like, "How did you physically feel?" to help the victim orient themselves to the facts.

Victims should be reminded that there are common reactions to an abusive situation, including losing hope for the future, feeling distant (ie, detached) or losing a sense of concern about others, difficulty with concentration or being able to make decisions, feeling jumpy and getting startled easily at sudden noises, feeling on guard and alert all the time, having dreams and memories that are upsetting, struggling at work or school, and a desire to avoid people, places, and things related to the event. Providers should connect them with community resources for counseling, coping strategies, and advocacy (eg, housing, safety planning, and communication). They will need support for getting a protective order or a restraining order through the courthouse.

Additional Resources

If you or someone you care about is experiencing dating violence, there are hotlines available 24 hours a day, 7 days a week, 365 days a year. Victims can call 1-800-899-4000 to speak with a trained advocate about their situation, or they can call any of the other numbers listed below.

— **National Domestic Violence Hotline:**

Thehotline.org

(1) 800-799-7233

TTY- (1) 800-787-3224

— **RAINN:**

Rainn.org

(1) 800-656-4673

Online Chat

— **Suicide Prevention Lifeline:**

988lifeline.org

(1) 800-273-8255

Call or Text 988

Online Chat

— **Trevor Lifeline:**

Thetrevorproject.org

(1) 866-488-7386

Chat and Text

— **Crisis Text Line:**

Crisistextline.org

Text HOME to 741741

Connected with crisis counselor

References

1. Dating violence. United States Department of Justice, Office on Violence Against Women. 2021. Accessed September 27, 2021. https://www.justice.gov/ovw/dating-violence

2. Violence against women. World Health Organization. Updated March 25, 2024. https://www.who.int/news-room/fact-sheets/detail/violence-against-women

3. Heise L, Garcia Moreno C. Violence by intimate partners. In: Krug EG, Dahlberg LL, Mercy JA, et al, eds. *World Report on Violence and Health*. World Health Organization; 2002:87-121.

4. Six different types of abuse. Reach Beyond Domestic Violence. 2021. https://reachma.org/blog/6-different-types-of-abuse/

5. Power and control. National Domestic Violence Hotline. https://www.thehotline.org/identify-abuse/power-and-control/

6. Breiding M, Basile K, Smith S, Black M, Rashema M. Intimate partner violence surveillance uniform definitions and recommended data elements. Centers for Disease Control and Prevention. 2015. https://www.cdc.gov/intimate-partner-violence/communication-resources/intimatepartnerviolence.pdf?CDC_AAref_Val=https://www.cdc.gov/violenceprevention/pdf/ipv/intimatepartnerviolence.pdf

7. Statistics. National Coalition Against Domestic Violence. 2024. https://ncadv.org/statistics

8. White SJ, Sin J, Mantovani N, et al. Global prevalence and mental health outcomes of intimate partner violence among women: a systematic review and meta-analysis. *Trauma Violence Abuse.* 2024;25(1):494-511. doi:10.1177/15248380231155529

9. Teen dating violence. National Institute of Justice. Accessed September 27, 2021. https://nij.ojp.gov/topics/crimes/teen-dating-violence

10. Domestic violence statistics. National Domestic Violence Hotline. Accessed September 27, 2021. https://www.thehotline.org/stakeholders/domestic-violence-statistics/

11. Prevalence of teen dating violence. National Institute of Justice. 2011. Accessed June 13, 2022. https://nij.ojp.gov/topics/articles/prevalence-teen-dating-violence

12. Espelage D, Low S, Anderson C, De La Ru L. Bullying, sexual, and dating violence trajectories from early to late adolescence. National Institute of Justice. April 21, 2014. https://www.ojp.gov/pdffiles1/nij/grants/246830.pdf

13. Clayton HB, Kilmer G, DeGue SA, et al. Dating violence, sexual violence, and bullying victimization among high school students- youth risk behavior survey, United States, 2021. *MMWR Supplements.* 2023;72(1):66-74. doi:10.15585/mmwr.su7201a8

14. Nahapetyan L, Orpinas P, Song X, et al. Longitudinal association of suicidal ideation and physical dating violence among high school students. *J Youth Adolesc.* 2014;43(4):629-640. doi:10.1007/s10964-013-0006-6

15. White J, Koss M. Courtship violence: incidence and prevalence in a national sample of higher education students. *Violence Vict.* 1991;6(4):247-256.

16. Hall Smith P, White J, Holland L. A longitudinal perspective on dating violence among adolescent and college-age women. *Am J Public Health.* 2003;93(7):1104-1109. doi:10.2105/AJPH.93.7.1104

17. Relationship abuse during the transition from adolescence to young adulthood. National Institute of Justice. Updated August 27, 2017. Accessed September 27, 2021. https://nij.ojp.gov/topics/articles/relationship-abuse-during-transition-adolescence-young-adulthood

18. Warning signs for college-age adults. RAINN. https://www.rainn.org/articles/warning-signs-college-age-adults

19. Shorey RC, Tirone V, Stuart GL. Coordinated community response components for victims of intimate partner violence: a review of the literature. *Aggress Violent Behav.* 2014;19(4):363-371. doi:10.1016/j.avb.2014.06.001

20. If you see something, say something. US Department of Homeland Security. https://www.dhs.gov/see-something-say-something

21. Anemone. Accessed June 13, 2022. http://www.anemoneapp.io/

22. Reid J, Haskell R, Dillahunt-Aspillaga C, Thor J. Trauma bonding and interpersonal violence. In: Van Leeuwen T, Brouwer M, eds. *Psychology of Trauma*. Nova Science Publishers; 2013.

Section II

Assessment

Assessment Questions

Chapter 2: A Historical Perspective

1. Which of the following terms have been used to describe interpersonal violence?

   A. Crimes against women

   B. Domestic violence

   C. Gender-based violence

   D. Intimate partner violence

   E. Relationship violence

   F. All of the above

2. Which cultural society enacted the first laws in the world against wife-beating and unnatural severity to children?

   A. Native Americans

   B. Puritans

   C. Roman Empire

3. Why have Native American communities struggled to get justice for cases of interpersonal violence?

   A. There is confusion about jurisdiction between indigenous, local, and state law enforcement and court systems.

   B. There is an abundance of law enforcement and social resources available to people living on reservations.

   C. During European colonization, Native Americans were forced into a more patriarchal society, and land was allotted to men as required in the Dawes act.

4. During the 1960s and 1970s, what type of programs were developed to help women free themselves from abusive relationships?

   A. Domestic violence shelters

   B. International Tribunal on Crimes Against Women

   C. No-fault divorce laws

   D. Laws to prohibit discrimination against women in employment (equal pay for equal work)

   E. Take Back the Night anti-violence rallies

   F. All of the above

Chapter 3: Risk Factors for Experiencing Interpersonal Violence

1. What are 3 developmental characteristics from Table 3-1 that can increase a person's risk for experiencing interpersonal violence?
2. What types of childhood experiences predict a higher risk of interpersonal violence in future adult relationships?
3. What are some ways that health care personnel can support people who are experiencing interpersonal violence?

Chapter 4: General Indicators of Interpersonal Violence in Women's Health

1. A pregnant woman is at an even greater risk of physical abuse.
   A. True
   B. False
2. Domestic violence refers to:
   A. Abuse that only women can experience
   B. Hitting and physical abuse only
   C. Most types of sexual abuse
   D. Violence among intimate partners
3. Which of the following statements is true regarding sexual orientation and indicators of domestic violence?
   A. Help-seeking behavior among males experiencing DV may be lowered because of fear of disclosure.
   B. Gay men are largely unaffected by domestic violence.
   C. Male partners in same-sex relationships pose a lesser risk for DV than female partners in same-sex relationships.
   D. Same-sex intimate partner violence (SSIPV) is comparable to rates identified in heterosexual relationships.

Chapter 5: LGBTQIA+ Considerations

1. LGBTQIA+ individuals face increased disrespect and discrimination when seeking health care services.
   A. True
   B. False
2. All of the following are types of abuse associated with LGBTQIA+ individuals EXCEPT:
   A. Targeting a partner's genitals or chest
   B. Denying a partner access to hormones
   C. Damaging gender expression clothing
   D. Identity theft
   E. Using words for a partner's body parts that align with their gender identity

3. Match each phrase to the term it defines

    A. Cisgender

    B. Gender queer

    C. Heterosexism

    D. Homophobia

    E. Nonbinary

    F. Transphobia

        i. A person whose gender identity is something other than male or female

        ii. The systemic oppression of transgender people because they do not fit society's expectations of what men and women are supposed to act and look like

        iii. The systemic oppression of gay men, lesbians, and bisexual people because of their sexuality

        iv. A person whose gender identity corresponds to the gender assigned at birth

        v. The belief that heterosexual relationships and people are the ideal and that they are better or more "normal" than queer relationships and people

        vi. A transgender or gender nonconforming person who identifies outside of the male/female gender binary

Chapter 6: Domestic Violence in the Military Setting

1. List at least 3 stressors unique to the military that increase the risk of IPV.
2. Name 2 to 3 barriers to care that IPV victims face in the military.
3. What is the Family Advocacy Program Directive?

Chapter 7: Identification and Response to Interpersonal Violence in the Health Care Setting

1. A patient should not be discharged without asking interpersonal violence screening questions, even if it means asking the questions in front of someone else.

    A. True

    B. False

2. Reasons that health care providers may not feel equipped to ask interpersonal violence screening questions are:

    A. They have not been trained on interpersonal violence.

    B. They do not have anywhere to refer patients if they disclose abuse.

    C. They are concerned that they will not have time to respond if the patient discloses.

    D. All of the above

Chapter 8: The Economical and Societal Impacts

1. Name 3 possible corollary victims of interpersonal violence.
2. Which type of housing offers the victim counseling services?
   A. Emergency
   B. Transitional
3. The victim incurs the largest financial burden of direct costs from interpersonal violence.
   A. True
   B. False
4. Name 4 effects interpersonal violence has on children.
5. Businesses are largely unaffected by interpersonal violence.
   A. True
   B. False

Chapter 9: Stalking and Interpersonal Violence

1. Define *stalking,* and list common practices of a stalker.
2. What are the 3 diagnostic categories of stalkers?
3. List at least 2 typical examples of cyberstalking.

Chapter 10: Dating Violence Among High School and College Students

1. What are the different types of dating violence/abuse?
2. What actions can parents take to help their child(ren) handle teen/college dating violence? Provide at least 2 answers to each of the following questions.
   A. What can schools do?
   B. What can students do?
3. Approximately 1 in 10 high school students experience physical violence in a dating relationship.
   A. True
   B. False

Section III

Answer Key

Chapter 2

1. F
2. B
3. A
4. F

Chapter 3

1. Possible answers include: low self-esteem and depression in females, alcohol abuse, illegal substance use.
2. Possible answers include: witnessing interpersonal violence as a child, parental separation or divorce, physical abuse.
3. Possible answers include: performing risk assessments, discussing resources with patients, encourage and facilitate change of modifiable risk factors.

Chapter 4

1. A
2. D
3. D

Chapter 5

1. A
2. E
3. A. Cisgender (iv): A person whose gender identity corresponds to the gender assigned at birth

   B. Gender queer (i): A person whose gender identity is something other than male or female

   C. Heterosexism (v): The belief that heterosexual relationships and people are the ideal and that they are better or more "normal" than queer relationships and people

   D. Homophobia (iii): The systemic oppression of gay men, lesbians, and bisexual people because of their sexuality

   E. Nonbinary (vi): A transgender or gender nonconforming person who identifies outside of the male/female gender binary

   F. Transphobia (ii): The systemic oppression of transgendered people because they do not fit society's expectations of what men and women are supposed to act and look like

Chapter 6

1. Possible answers include: isolation, absence of support by extended family, trauma/PTSD, marital inequality, financial dependence, etc.
2. Possible answers include: lack of resources or knowledge of resources, frequent moves, lack of communication between care systems, fear of reporting due to perpetrator consequences or loss of finances if perpetrator is convicted, social stigma, fear that the perpetrator will be favored in legal proceedings, etc.
3. The directive requires each branch of the US Armed Forces to implement the Family Advocacy Program, which aims to address and prevent child maltreatment and spousal abuse. It includes a safe and confidential place to report abuse, a confidential registry to collect and analyze data associated with its services, and a case review committee, among others.

Chapter 7

1. B. False – If interpersonal violence screening questions cannot be asked when the patient is alone, it is better not to ask.
2. D

Chapter 8

1. Children, family members, friends, law enforcement officers, and strangers
2. B
3. B
4. Anxiety, increased fear, depression, nightmares, regressive behaviors, aggression, anger, appetite changes, isolation, increased fighting behaviors, falling grades, diabetes, obesity, heart disease, future abusive relationships, addictive behaviors
5. B

Chapter 9

1. A course of conduct involving repeated actions, which must occur on more than 1 occasion. Common behaviors include following victims, giving gifts, vandalizing property, photographing victims or their families, and physical and/or sexual assault.
2. Simple obsessional, love obsessional, and erotomaniac
3. Possible answers include: sending repeated unsolicited emails and instant messages, subscribing the victim to services, committing identity theft, impersonating another online.

Chapter 10

1. Physical abuse, sexual abuse, psychological harm, verbal/emotional abuse, financial/economic abuse, cultural/identity abuse
2. Possible answers include: build trusting relationships, communicate with their children about who they are dating and socializing with outside of school, be aware of their children's whereabouts, monitor their children's welfare.

   A. What can schools do?

   Possible answers include: document suspected/reported abuse and notify parents, police, and the Department of Health and Human Services; reporting systems for students such as "See Something, Say Something," incorporate dating violence education into curriculum.

B. What can students do?

Possible answers include: develop a crisis plan and share with trusted adults, discuss with parents/teachers about identifying abuse tactics, report abuse or suspected abuse to a trusted adult.

3. A

www.ingramcontent.com/pod-product-compliance
Lightning Source LLC
Chambersburg PA
CBHW061356240926
51846CB00007B/1421